When Your Library Budget
Is Almost Zero

When Your Library Budget Is Almost Zero

Lesley S. J. Farmer

1993
LIBRARIES UNLIMITED, INC.
Englewood, Colorado

Dedicated to my mother:
My first teacher and budget expert.

LIBRARIES UNLIMITED, INC.
P.O. Box 6633
Englewood, CO 80155-6633

Library of Congress Cataloging-in-Publication Data

Farmer, Lesley S. J.
    When your library budget is almost zero / Lesley S. J. Farmer.
    xi, 125 p. 17x25 cm.
    Includes bibliographical references.
    ISBN 0-87287-990-9
    1. Libraries--United States--Finance. I. Title.
Z683.2.U6F37 1993
025.1'1--dc20   93-20459
                                                CIP

CONTENTS

PREFACE

"I try to keep up with the library trends. I read about CD-ROM and know it would be great for my kids. But my library doesn't even have a telephone!"

"I put in a lean budget for the year, and my supervisor gave me only 10 percent of my request!"

"My principal told me that maybe we had enough books, that maybe we should review what we had, period."

"California's Proposition 13 was bad enough. Now the state budget looks so bleak, there's no more room to cut back."

Most librarians have a vision of what they want to accomplish in their libraries, but too often the vision is blurred by reality, particularly the reality of financial constraints. While preparing this book I read the following:

"What with all of the budget cuts we will be making for this next school year, I think we should take the $14,000 we have allocated for the salary of a librarian and spend it on materials to be placed in classrooms where they will be used." This statement, while it smacks of early 1950s administrator mentality, is very much a reality in the 1982-83 school year.[1]

Remember the U.S. recession in the early 1980s? The economy is not strong now in the 1990s, and libraries certainly are not given first priority in many places.

Although few libraries with inordinate amounts of money exist, a decreasing number of libraries are operating with adequate budgets; most libraries, especially small ones, need more money in order to do their jobs at a base level.

The original title of this book was *When Your Library Budget Is Zero*, but it sounded too extreme. Not anymore. Book sales to small libraries are down. Buildings are deteriorating. Staffs are being reduced or eliminated. Despite the White House Conference on Libraries and Information Service recommendations, federal spending on libraries is being cut.

This is dismal news, yet librarians can do something about it. They can still look for opportunities to serve their populations. They need not give up the ship! Rather, they can behave even more proactively. That is why one suggested subtitle of this book was *Financial Guerrilla Tactics in the Library Trenches, or What to Do Until Your Library Ship Comes In*.

Such an attitude is not Pollyannaish. It is a very realistic approach when the environment, be it in house or international, restricts library budgets. It is also a workable strategy when the problem may be the library itself. In either case, librarians need to look at what is happening "out there" as well as within their libraries.

They need to find out why their budgets are low or inadequate and decide what changes are under their control. With this information, librarians can plan a realistic course of action. Who knows? Maybe the rowboat can be traded in for a yacht! Or once the barnacles are scraped off, the librarian may see the library yacht that was there all along.

If we assume that librarians want to change the status quo of their libraries and want more than to just make do, this book is a practical guide for librarians who have a small staff and a shrinking budget.

The first chapter deals with planning: knowing where you are, where you want to go, and how to get there. The second chapter is a discussion about using space effectively and improving existing facilities as one approach to enhancing the existing situation. Even without a budget the librarian is usually expected to develop and maintain the collection. So the third chapter covers collection development and maintenance, as well as resource sharing. Because computers are high-profile items in terms of both demand and cost, the fourth chapter deals with their acquisition and use. Often a limited budget cuts out valuable staffing or staff time. The fifth chapter covers how to use volunteer help without undermining professional work. Included are suggestions for developing and involving interest groups and support networks. Several aspects of library service are covered in chapter 6: information retrieval, instruction, packaging information, and programs. Librarians can highlight the activities and potential of their libraries to justify larger budgets. Chapter 7 considers the opportunities of an ongoing public-relations effort and outlines effective methods. Although libraries should not run on "soft" funding, occasional fund-raising can help in focused areas or in temporary situations. Chapter 8 tells how librarians can implement and capitalize on fund-raising. The final chapter is more than a happy ending. When budgets are increased, librarians should plan for accompanying improvements and should immediately lay the groundwork for future budget expansion.

When your library budget is almost zero, the prospects may seem dim. When others are in the same boat, you may feel even more tied to your leaky rowboat. Hopefully, this book will provide a life ring to help you swim against the current and survive until you can captain your own sleek library.

NOTE

[1]William Pichette, "Protecting the Budget — and Your Position, Too!" *Book Report* (January 1983): 20.

1

Planning

safari hat for
missionary zeal

The Mission Statement,
kept in clear
visionary view

survival kit
to get through
the tough times

...and presented
to decision-makers
on a (borrowed)
silver platter

planner book

portable time
management
system

boots to wade through red tape

What would the ideal library be for you and for your potential users? Realistically, what would you like to see accomplished in the library? Although libraries must operate in light of their governing body's mission, it is librarians who set the tone for services and resources. It is the librarian's vision that provides clarity for library goals.

Without a mission and a vision, the library has no direction. By envisioning an achievable idea and examining the reality of the present, the librarian can determine the resultant gap and describe the actual needs of the library and its users. This evaluation process leads to effective planning that can provide a solid base for change—for the better.

THE MISSION STATEMENT

Mission statements have become almost trendy. They are hailed by marketing specialists and restructuring gurus as the basis for all-ensuing discussion and planning. A reason exists for such advocacy: Mission statements really do work.

Briefly, a mission statement is "a precise, concise and inspiring declaration of the fundamental purpose for which the organization exists. Who are we and what is supposed to happen for whom as a result of what we do?"[1] A mission statement focuses on action and defines specific strategies needed to accomplish critical goals. It is also the basis for evaluation: Did the library achieve what it set out to do? A good mission statement keeps a library from staying in a rut; it looks around and ahead rather than backward.

Certainly the mission statement within the American Association of School Librarians' and Association for Educational Communications and Technology's *Information Power* is an exemplary place to start: "The mission of the library media program is to ensure that students and staff are effective users of ideas and information."[2] The American Library Association's Library Bill of Rights is another inspiration for creating an exciting library mission statement. Other not-for-profit organizations such as the Girl Scouts have effective mission statements that are useful to study.

The mission statement should reflect the ideas of those parties who influence the library or are influenced by it: the governing body, library staff, and users. A good way to proceed is to have a small representative group of people consider these questions:

- Why does the library exist?

- What is your immediate image of the library and what it stands for?

- Whom does the library serve?

- What makes the library distinctive?

- What key words about the library have meaningful connotations?

- How will the library achieve its goals?

As the group examines the responses, it is hoped that some patterns will emerge that capture the spirit of the library. Those patterns then become the basis for developing a mission statement.

Suppose there is a gap between what the library does now and what it should do. Maybe the library's image is that of a study hall. At the other extreme is the image of the perfect library with unlimited staffing, facilities, resources, and money; such perfection could not be achieved. The message is, Don't go to extremes. The mission statement should reflect a realistic ideal: the best that the library can do within its actual environment and with its existing or achievable resources.

Once a workable mission statement is developed, it can be used as the basis for evaluating and planning. Librarians should realize that after looking at all the factors involved, the mission statement may look unrealistic. Remember that it is not written in stone. It should be flexible enough to continue to reflect the achievable goals of the library.

WHAT IS HAPPENING IN THE LIBRARY?

The next step is to take a careful look at the library and its environment. A vital part of dealing with a constrained budget is to evaluate and plan in order to make sound decisions, make the best use of an existing budget, and achieve the goals set for the library. Librarians need to know what is happening, why it is happening, what needs to change in order to improve, and what difference evaluation and ensuing change make in terms of the budget.

Because the evaluation objectives shape the process and success of effective budget management, the first question librarians need to ask as they evaluate is, What level of service do I want to achieve in line with the mission statement? It is probably best to target a couple of specific issues such as student outcomes or collection use.

Because the evaluation is being used to manage and increase library budgets, the choice of measurement tools, evaluators, and types of questions will reflect that perspective. For instance, the librarian might focus on the collection and ask users how successfully they can find the materials they seek, using a reference fill rate questionnaire (see figure 1.1). A follow-up evaluation activity might ask users open-ended questions about the kinds of materials they would like to have included in the library.

One important reason to evaluate is to find out what users want (or think they want) and need (or think they need). The differences between wants and needs, in terms of both the users' and the librarian's perceptions, are crucial in serving the people who walk into the library.

Probably the most complex part of the evaluation process involves choosing the appropriate measurement tool. Major factors influence one's choice: format, evaluatee, evaluator, time, and financial or other limitations. Particularly with constrained budgets, the measurement tool should be inexpensive and quick, easy to administer and analyze, and as neutral and objective as possible. Some sample formats that could be used for budget-based evaluations include

- questionnaires to measure opinions. They can include multiple-choice items or free-response questions.

- rating scales to assess relative strengths. For example, these can rate the quality of space allocation from 1 to 10.

Fig. 1.1. Materials Availability Survey Form. From Van House, Nancy, et al. *Output Measures for Public Libraries: A Manual of Standardized Procedures.* 2d ed. Chicago: American Library Association, 1987.

Form number _____

LIBRARY SURVEY

Library _____   Date _____

PLEASE FILL OUT THIS SURVEY AND RETURN IT AS YOU LEAVE.

We want to know if you find what you look for in our libraries. Please list below what you looked for today. Mark "YES" if you found it, and "NO" if you did not find it.

TITLE

If you are looking for a specific book, record, cassette, newspaper, or issue of a magazine, please write the title below. Include any reserve material picked up.

NAME OF WORK (Example) • Gone with the Wind	FOUND? YES NO
1.	
2.	
3.	
4.	
5.	

SUBJECT OR AUTHOR

If you are looking for materials or information on a particular subject or a special author today, please note each subject or person below.

SUBJECT OR AUTHOR (Examples) • how to repair a toaster • any book by John D. MacDonald	DID YOU FIND SOMETHING? YES NO
1.	
2.	
3.	
4.	
5.	

BROWSING
If you were browsing and not looking for anything specific, did you find something of interest?

YES _____   NO _____

OTHER
_____ Check here if your visit today did *not* include any of the above activities. (Example) using the photocopy machine.

COMMENTS We would appreciate any comments on our service and collections on the back of this sheet.

THANK YOU!

- semantic differentials to measure attitudes. For example, a survey might include items such as:
  "Rushed Staff − − − − − − − − − − Inactive Staff."

- observations to evaluate events firsthand. Try to be unobtrusive.

- interviews to get in-depth and sensitive information.

WHAT IS HAPPENING OUTSIDE THE LIBRARY?

Because no library operates in a vacuum, librarians must look at the external forces as well as the internal state. Once external threats and opportunities are identified and analyzed, then librarians can analyze their own libraries and take appropriate action.

Basically, external forces are those factors beyond the librarian's direct control: political, technological, economic, social, competitive. For example the library might have to report to an adversarial town council: a desirable technology such as cable television might not be locally available; a business may have to close down its research and development division; the state might have a budget shortfall that affects the library; the local population might not be highly educated; competing schools might vie for students and money.

External forces can impact libraries significantly and must be included in overall strategic planning. If external forces are in the library's favor, such as a newly appointed board member who loves books, then the librarian should take advantage of that external windfall. If the external force is negative, such as a poor neighborhood, then the librarian should not ask for monetary donations so much as donations of time.

ANALYZING THE FINDINGS

Information is important, but only through interpreting that information can librarians develop feasible plans to deal with constrained budgets. Basically, the analysis involves finding patterns or trends in the data collected and then pursuing the important question: Why? For example, do users tend to find the materials they are looking for? If the answer is yes, the reason may be a good collection, good access tools, librarian intervention, or even low expectations. A no answer may indicate inadequate library skills, an inadequate collection, too high a circulation rate, unrealistic expectations, poor space management, or even poor lighting or eyesight.

Some trends may be easy to interpret, such as low circulation of science books and the fact that 80 percent of those books are more than 10 years old. But the connection between the size of facility and the quality of bibliographic instruction may be coincidental. When trends arise but the cause is unknown, follow-up evaluation is needed.

DEVELOPING STRATEGIES

Why does a gap exist between the current library situation and the library's goals? Once the librarian uses solid evaluation methods to discover the reason, effective solutions can be formulated to bridge the library gap. Are users unaware of services and resources? Then educate the constituents and start a public-relations campaign. Do users have low expectations? Then improve public relations, increase service in one target area, and model high-level expectations and fulfillment. Is staffing inadequate? Show what could be done with proper personnel. Use volunteers and encourage them to become professionally trained.

Librarians also need to determine whether the budget gap is a temporary problem or a long-term situation. If budget difficulties are short term and beyond library control, the librarian may be able to ride out the wave and regroup. If the problem is significant and not time sensitive or externally controlled, then a thorough plan of action is required.

If budgetary limitations are a major factor of the gap between ideal and actual libraries, librarians need to concentrate on factors within their control (though being mindful of external forces) and to develop feasible strategies.

Prioritize services and resources. Doing one job well, developing one portion of the collection satisfactorily, or providing one successful program accomplishes more than does a watered-down version of inclusive service. A focused approach provides a model of performance and results that would be possible in expanded form with adequate financial support.

Fight selectively. If many problems and obstacles occur, choose which ones are worth battling. Demonstrating a willingness to negotiate and compromise reduces psychological barriers. Demanding high standards for worthy projects demonstrates the librarian's values and priorities.

Find alternative routes. If administrators block the way, work directly with faculty. If board members show little support, look for support from users. If collection development is curtailed, concentrate on instruction.

Evangelize. Rather than groan about what cannot be done, find ways to show what is possible. Share achievements in the library and raise expectations. Show what miracles can happen in a well-supported library. Show how libraries can make a difference.

Look around. Find out what other libraries are doing. Gather ideas. Get support. Keep an open mind and a broad perspective.

Become indispensable. Make the library the center of the school or community. Imagine life without a photocopier or a telephone. Analogously, ensure that resources and services attain such a status that pulling the library "plug" would stop the educational process.

As the previous examples illustrate, strategic planning can take many forms. Strategies may focus on perceptual changes, on making people aware of different perspectives rather than on changing library services. Strategies may involve altering attitudes or increasing expectations. Strategy may deal with structural changes: scheduling time differently, incorporating information skills across the curriculum, modifying staff functions.

Because participants in the evaluation expect results soon after the process is completed, librarians need to determine what changes can be implemented within, say, a month. One simple action can symbolize the usefulness of an evaluation. Perhaps the librarian can buy or borrow lounge pillows for a quiet youth corner, create some attractive signs, or introduce a weekly video program. These new features are concrete and underline the librarian's willingness to improve the library within a limited budget.

Regardless of the strategies planned, librarians need to communicate their efforts to all who will be affected. Memos, announcements, newsletters, displays, word of mouth should all be used to reinforce the message that evaluation makes a difference. Foremost should be the mission statement directing the plan.

Librarians need not act as lone voices in the wilderness. They should build a supportive constituency to carry the message forward. The final strategy plan should have a broad-based "ownership" in order to facilitate action and enlist adequate support.

A BRIEF WORD ABOUT BUDGETING

Once a strong strategic plan is developed, the detailed work of preparing a realistic budget must be pursued. With constrained funding, budgeting may seem simple: no money, no expenses. However, the same thoughtfulness that goes into managing a well-endowed library needs to be applied to an austere case. A realistic budget shows the library's health and the costs of library objectives, identifies resources, shows the relationship between program and decisions, plans work, states expectations, and communicates.[3]

Before a budget is laid out, the librarian must gather data about user needs, available resources, and library goals. Rather than using an across-the-board percentage cut, librarians would be wise to use a zero-based approach where each program area is analyzed and allocated. The key word is *prioritize*. What are the essential services of the library, and what can be subordinated in light of its mission statement?

Detailed budgeting for any service includes several factors: time, resources, staffing. Cost-effectiveness is another consideration: What is the return service value for each dollar expended? The librarian should also consider alternative ways to meet the service goal — and determine the costs of each of them.

Mention should also be made of the distinction between capital and consumable spending. Capital expenditures, for books and equipment as examples, can be depreciated over time. Not enough governing bodies take these items into account as they should.

Of course, once a budget is drawn up, it should be presented. This task also takes skill. Here are a few pointers:

- Focus on who the decisionmakers are.

- Choose the timing for the most positive reception.

- Keep documentation clear, concise, organized, and professional looking.

- Use charts and graphs for easy reading.

- Focus on the mission statement.

- Defend the budget by program rather than by line items.

- Clearly state specific program priorities.

- Identify ahead of time those items or programs that could be questioned and develop points to defend those costs, if needed.

- Point out those services that can be improved without increased spending.

- Show sources of revenue or gifts in kind.

- Highlight internal and external factors influencing the budget.

- Consider in-house paybacks for extra library services such as videotaping, duplicating, or telecommunications. (This approach is used more often in special libraries, where departments keep detailed records of each job. Look to the governing body for precedence rather than initiating paybacks as a new budgetary procedure.)

- Be prepared to negotiate; know which areas are open for discussion and which are worth fighting for.

However the presentation goes, be sure to thank participants for listening. If suggestions have been given to revise the budget, incorporate them as well and as quickly as possible, bearing in mind the library's mission statement and priority services. The main general advice is to maintain and communicate a highly professional image.

WORKING SMARTER

A tight budget challenges the librarian to work smarter. The library has to become a lean, mean machine. Productivity has to be even higher given the budget restraints. What are some ways to trim the fat without bleeding?

Study and implement time management skills. Look at the tasks being done and not being done, then prioritize them according to goals.

Standardize. Exceptions take time and mental effort. Examine existing library rules and procedures to see if they are effective. For instance, if four different circulation periods exist, cut them down to two. Handle all requests the same way. Write a clear manual of procedures to ensure consistency and share it with all involved.

Simplify. Cut out any extraneous business. Use forms whenever possible: checklists, overdues, magazine requests, schedules. Instead of writing a response letter, photocopy the original and write the reply in the margins.

Analyze tasks. This activity may smack of scientific management, so use all staff, including volunteers, as task sleuths. Then looking at the most efficient way (i.e., with least time and least cost) to do a task becomes enjoyable. Is the distance between supplies and books too great? Is some subtask, such as typing names, done several times when it could be done once?

Train others. As more people know how to do more jobs, they can substitute for each other. Those jobs requiring less than professional training should be done by aides and volunteers; the initial time put in to train dependable people will more than pay off in terms of time management and in terms of library support.

Be creative. Have marked, open-end shelves so that students can return books close to the right stack instead of misfiling them or leaving them on the tables. If teachers have preparation times, have them work in the library as serious role models to cut down on noise monitoring (assuming the teacher is quiet). Let outside groups conduct free programs in the library during off hours.

LEADERSHIP

This kind of active evaluation, planning, and management requires real library leadership. A passive attitude has no place in crisis times and is, in fact, counterproductive.

It is hoped that budget-limited librarians have good relationships with their staff so that they can build morale and cohesiveness within the group. If human relationships are marginal, then an authoritative attitude must be taken. Otherwise, the staff will be nonproductive and scattered.

Whether other staff exist or not, budget-constrained librarians need to exhibit strong leadership: Such skills do not cost money, but the lack of such skills is very costly in terms of library effectiveness. What is called for is a clear direction with focused attention, clear and enthusiastic communication, and an atmosphere of trust, reliability, and accomplishments. Even with a small budget, a library with a strong self-image and a supportive, collaborative spirit can easily build effective coalitions.[4]

NOTES

[1]Glenn H. Tecker, *Symposium for Chief Elected Officers and Chief Staff Executives* (Washington, D.C.: American Society of Association Executives), 118.

[2]American Association of School Librarians and the Association for Educational Communications and Technology, *Information Power: Guidelines for School Library Media Programs* (Chicago: American Library Association, 1988), 1.

[3]Ann E. Prentice, *Financial Planning for Libraries.* (Metuchen, N.J.: Scarecrow, 1983), 27.

[4]Tecker, 103.

CHAPTER

2

Facilities

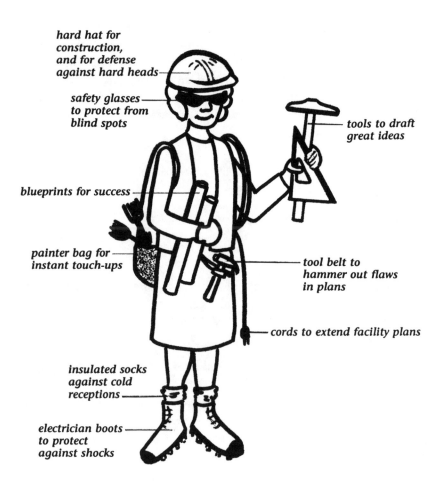

hard hat for
construction,
and for defense
against hard heads

safety glasses
to protect from
blind spots

tools to draft
great ideas

blueprints for success

painter bag for
instant touch-ups

tool belt to
hammer out flaws
in plans

cords to extend facility plans

insulated socks
against cold
receptions

electrician boots
to protect
against shocks

Using space efficiently is one significant way to improve the existing budget-constrained situation. It not only helps productivity but also improves morale. A well-organized, comfortable library, small though it may be, speaks well for the librarian. Even cosmetic changes can change attitudes and behavior. Librarians would do well to examine decorating books, especially of apartment spaces, to get inspired about library-space management.

WORKING WITH AVAILABLE SPACE

Often space limitations reflect budget limitations. In those cases, creative ways to work within a small area are needed. Several approaches can be used: making space do double duty, dividing existing space, rearranging space, and finding alternative space.

Closet libraries are common, often containing a small collection kept under lock and key by a teacher. If the library is more than a warehouse for books, library space might be shared by two departments. A larger area may include shelving mainly for library materials, with table space available for instruction by the librarian and another resource teacher. The following combinations have been successful in schools:

- library and computer instruction;

- library and resource specialist; and

- library and ESL (English as a second language) instruction (though noisy).

In one case, the library was housed in the far end of an assembly room! Three issues must be resolved between the cooperating teacher and the librarian: class scheduling, supervision of materials, and storage of classroom teacher materials.

When the library has exclusive use of an enclosed space, double duty of space is still possible. A school library workroom, traditionally reserved for processing materials, may be shared by students and faculty for AV (audiovisual) production, school publications, tutoring, and other school activities. In one case, the workroom was the quietest place for students to study! In one library a side room was used to house college information. Using long carrels, the librarian created a separate area within the room for listening to music and for casual group work. In another instance, a small area around the corner from the main library space was used for leisure reading and for small programs such as poetry reading. The cozy atmosphere contributed to its double-duty success.

Side rooms adjoining libraries can be a real boon as spaces for computers and typewriters, AV production, professional collections, library instruction, classroom seminars. Oftentimes, these functions can overlap in one space. A sectioned-off reference area can be used for library instruction. In fact, if the library is divided visually by shelves or other furniture arrangement, those areas can be sites for library instruction about the surrounding types of information: magazines, computer-access tools, picture books. In one case, even the hall was used between periods as a space to show videos!

Another way to magically expand space is to divide it. By shifting shelves and tables, differentiated library functions can be established: reference, leisure reading, small-group work, individual study, storytelling. Waist-high shelving is particularly effective because it ensures good supervision and a sense of room spaciousness while it encircles a small group of users working with similar types of materials.

Movable dividers or screens can separate short-term groupings visually. These are useful when a class or interest group is using part of the library. Screen dividers with storybook characters on the panels create a cozy corner for groups of young users and storyteller listeners. Dividers can also block out some noise. When a space is divided regularly, a curtain or shade can be installed and used as needed. Other subtle ways to create smaller, differentiated spaces within a larger space include distinctive area rugs, different furniture groupings, different lighting levels, banners, and platforms.

Space division can evoke a chaotic feeling if not managed well. Therefore, when small-group areas are developed, an overall consistent look is necessary. Furniture should be the same color or style, walls should be the same color, and signage should look alike and be placed at the same height throughout the area. At the minimum, the library should communicate a consistent "feel," be it cozy, business-like, or light and airy.

Space can also be rearranged more efficiently. Consider remote storage areas for little-used but necessary items. Look for any dead areas such as entryways or corners. Can they be used for storage, display space, or study areas? The advantages of freer movement around stacks is more than compensated by the additional space available for shelving or carrels (figure 2.1). Check the library's traffic pattern. Do staff or users have to walk a long distance between similar functions or frequent tasks? How is noise distributed? The loudest point should be at the front, the quietest in the rear. At the minimum, separate noisy and quiet areas.

Fig. 2.1. Shelves arranged in a standard layout and in U-shaped bays.

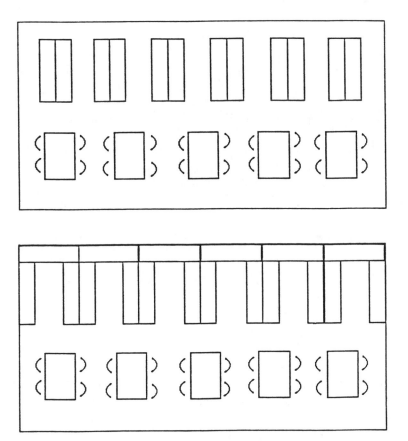

Examine shelf space. A couple of oversized books can force wider shelf spacing. Paperbacks can slip behind other books if deep shelving is used. Adjustable shelving is best to accommodate a variety of sizes, but even set shelves can be used efficiently (see figure 2.2). Having a single, integrated collection is ideal, but when space is at a premium, well-marked modifications for odd-sized books are workable. Oversized items can be placed together on a marked, bottom shelf for each range. Use dummy blocks of styrofoam or cardboard to mark the space of an oversized book and create a well-marked section of these oversized books. Shelve fiction paperbacks separately in narrower shelving. If that shelving is not contiguous to the hardback fiction area, make sure to have a sign pointing to the paperback section. Weed the collection assiduously!

Fig. 2.2. Intershelving of materials in various formats. Reprinted, with permission, from Jean Weihs, *Accessible Storage of Nonbook Materials* (Phoenix, AZ: Oryx, 1984), 14.

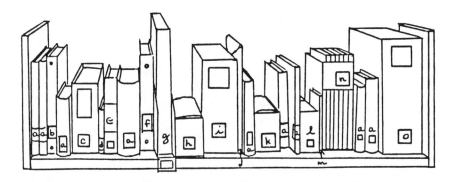

a. book; b. binder containing microfiches; c. box containing filmstrips; d. book-like album containing a single a sound cassette; e. videotape cassette in container; f. binder containing slides; g. clip-on holder containing a motion picture in a box; h. motion picture loop cartridge in container; i. box containing slide carousel; j. envelope containing a single Viewmaster slide; k. microfilm reel in container; l. box containing microopaque cards; m. pamphlet binder containing a single picture; n. Princeton file holding issues of a current periodical; o. kit housed in a box

Consider how closets are used. A closet can be transformed into office space, a sink area, a computer workstation, display space, a telephone booth, a puppet theater, or an audio center. Take advantage of a closet's locked door: It provides security for sensitive or expensive equipment, and narrow shelves on the door itself can be used for storing narrow items.

Consider the direction of the furniture. Try diagonals to improve supervision, to add novelty, or to improve traffic flow. Think modular. Think flexible. Movable furniture helps librarians change arrangements upon need.

In extreme cases, curriculum-based resource centers can house part of the collection. However, this approach has distinct disadvantages:

- Users have to look in more than one location for materials.

- Catalog cards need to be marked to identify the alternative location.

- Supervision in resource centers is often restricted.

- No professional help is available for finding information.

- A danger of duplicative acquisitions exists.

MAKING COSMETIC IMPROVEMENTS

Even with a limited budget, renovations are possible. Whether the issue is one of noise or storage, simple and inexpensive means exist to improve the library's look.

Reduce noise levels by

- using drapes as bulletin boards (pinning the display elements), dividers, or distinctive ceilings;

- stapling egg cartons together to create acoustical tile;

- lining computer-printer areas with carpet squares as sound buffers;

- using divider screens to block off sound.

Improve flooring by

- making a patchwork carpet made of carpet samples (ask suppliers for donations);

- using rug ends.

Add seating areas with

- carpet-sample squares for story time;

- portable work lapboards made of plywood;

- carrels created by interlocking large cardboard pieces and placing them on tables (fig. 2.3).

Fig. 2.3. Carrels created with interlocking cardboard.

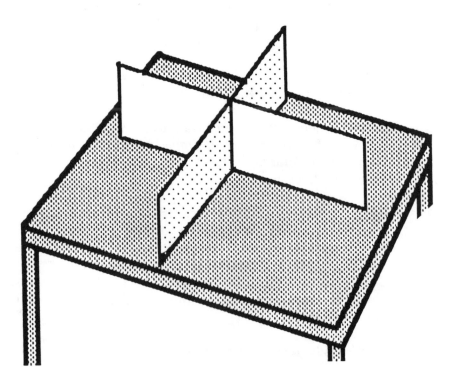

Introduce color through

- banners;

- kites (which businesses can donate);

- displays and posters;

- student-made murals;

- Japanese umbrellas;

- a bed sheet used as a big pinnable bulletin board;

- bed sheets looped across the ceiling for an exotic look;

- clear vinyl adhesive paper on the ends of bookshelf ranges;

- a patchwork wall of student work or old magazine covers;

- colorful divider screens, where panels are fabric or cardboard covered with artwork or old covers;

- spray-paint on boxes, baskets, poles, ends of bookshelf ranges, files;

- colorful window shades, especially if painted on (shades can also be used as an alternative to cabinet doors);

- maps;

- bright signage;

- open storage of storybook puppets;

- colorful pillows that serve as additional seating.

Note that color should be used as dramatic highlight. It is best to have broad areas of neutral color to unify the library and add the splashes of color to focus attention. Haphazard overuse of gaudy color creates a chaotic feeling.

Add display space using

- empty shelving;

- empty chairs;

- support poles;

- book carts;

- miniature stands (fig. 2.4);

Fig. 2.4. Miniature stands.

(List continues on next page.)

- banners suspended from the ceiling;

- mobiles;

- three-tiered hanging wire baskets;

- latticework;

- divider screens with fabric or cardboard sections;

- free-standing props such as baskets, trunks, sports equipment, toys, even umbrellas.

Add storage areas by

- hanging narrow items on the insides of doors (watch for slamming);

- finishing warehouse pallets and hanging newspapers on them;

- attaching window shades to unused top shelving in a children's library to create a hidden storage area;

- hanging items from a pegboard; children can each donate a clean sock in which to hold their list of assignments;

- using baskets, trunks, #10 cans, crates;

- cutting donated large cereal boxes at an angle on the sides to create Princeton files;

- using shelf tops as extra shelving. The main consideration when adding any shelving is to ensure logical arrangement so that users can find what they need easily.

Whenever possible storage areas should be out of the user's sight. The library's overall look should be organized, not cluttered and exposed.

TWO TRUE TALES

The many guises of a pencil holder. There is never a need to buy pencil holders with all the wonderful creative possibilities that surround the library:

- jars;

- covered cans and cardboard rolls—try making them into storybook characters (fig. 2.5);

Fig. 2.5. Storybook-character pencil holder.

- flower "frogs";

- chipped cups and vases;

- flower pots;

- child's rubber boot;

- cut-off plastic bottles;

- small boxes;

- bricks with holes.

This same principle of converting ordinary objects can be applied to containers for all sorts of supplies: art, office, AV. For those tippy containers, add a rock or clay to the bottom for extra weight.

The saga of a cardboard box. Cardboard boxes are a true staple of the library. Besides their normal use as containers for books, covered cardboard boxes can be transformed into

- poster containers — slide rolled-up posters into the partitions of a wine-bottle carton;

- containers for returning books, especially in other parts of a school during peak return periods;

- traveling-collection containers;

- program kits — include a thematic set of books, puppets or other props, bookmarks or other handouts, activity sheets or guides;

- the definitive recycling containers;

- dioramas;

- display bases — cover a group of different-height boxes with lively cloth, then display exciting books;

- kiosks or corner display stands — stack boxes (or cover the entire column with a bed sheet) and pin artwork on the faces of the boxes;

- cars of a train—join painted boxes either with the tops shut as a cute model or with the tops open to display books inside (being sure to paint the boxes' interiors as well);

- readers' hideaways—let little ones create their own private spaces, be it a boat, a house, or a cave, by painting a large sturdy box and adopting it as their own (fig. 2.6);

Fig. 2.6. Readers' hideaway.

- mazes—join open-ended, refrigerator-sized boxes together to create great tunnels for a fun program or fair activity;

- puppet theaters—cut a stage opening out of a refrigerator box that is open in the back;

- furniture—triple-thickness cardboard is stable enough to use as ersatz plywood;

- child-sized chairs and tables—paint sturdy, closed cardboard cubes;

- shelving—boxes with the open end on the side can be grouped together for primary books (watch for heavy, two-stacked loading!);

- file cabinets—turn one box on its side as the cabinet and store items in the top-open box (create a handle by cutting an elongated oval in the front of the storage box) (fig. 2.7);

- backboards or bulletin boards—cut large boxes and staple them to the back sides of open shelving;

- carrels—make a small one by turning a box on its side.

Fig. 2.7. File cabinet from a cardboard box.

One imaginative person cut a box on the diagonal to form an open wedge shape. Balloons covered the inside faces; a mesh covering was stapled to the edges to keep the balloons from escaping. Voila! instant party cushioned seat.

Cardboard is not a permanent solution but is useful for temporary situations. And it's ecological.

FURNITURE

Furniture is a major expense and should be approached seriously. It is better to have less furniture that is well suited to the library than to have a library crowded with substandard furniture that is underused. Extremely small libraries do well to invest in more books and shelving than in seating, because users can borrow most materials and take them elsewhere.

Worn furniture sometimes just needs refurbishing, but other times replacements are required. Any decision should take into account the length of time commitment (is this a stopgap measure?); immediacy of need; available human resources (what local craftspeople can work on the furniture?); and the financial situation, both short-term and long-term. Whatever the choice, quality should be the best possible for the materials used; shoddy work never pays. In particular, shelving must be able to withstand heavy loads.

A coat of paint can do wonders. High-gloss enamel, especially, can withstand hard wear. Nor does paint have to cost bundles. Besides the occasional paint sales, close-out sales and paint end-of-runs offer good prices. One facility placed an announcement in the local paper and received enough donated paint to take care of the entire exterior. One note of caution: Keep enough paint for future touch-ups.

Sometimes good-quality furniture can be made by library-friends groups or by vocational-education students. Examine their past work before commissioning them and get a cap cost for their efforts as well as a deadline date. Consider buying from refurbishing companies, who buy library furniture, repair and refurnish it, and sell it to other libraries at a reasonable cost. As a short-term solution, varnish hollow doors and use screw legs or sawhorses to hold up this kind of table.

Library and business liquidations, auctions, and bankruptcy sales offer another opportunity for low-cost purchases. A few points should be followed in order to get the best deal. Write a list of needed library items beforehand and include dimensions if appropriate. Occasionally an unexpected piece is too inexpensive and potentially useful to resist, but don't get stuck with an unnecessary item. Get to the site early and examine the merchandise closely for workmanship and wear. Be prepared. Know the retail price and set an upper budget limit. Unless the item is an extraordinary buy, keep to that limit even in the excitement of auctioning. Finally, know how to get purchases delivered and how to get them serviced. Rarely will any item be under warranty.

Surplus suppliers also offer bargains. The Federal Property Resources Services of the General Service Administration disposes of surplus items. The National Association for the Exchange of Industrial Resources is a not-for-profit group that matches industrial surplus to the needs of schools. Industrial equipment suppliers themselves sometimes have special discounts for libraries.

Good community relations also pay off. Bookstores and drugstores give away their display racks and other recyclables to loyal library customers. Locally based computer-user groups sometimes develop partnerships with schools or libraries, providing them with free or near-free equipment. When businesses upgrade their furniture or equipment, they give libraries their usable items as tax write-offs. In one case, a computer software company donated a new program for a school raffle; when no one won the raffle, it was given to the school library.

Lastly, library friends can make donations. If the librarian has a comprehensive list of needed furniture, those members who don't have the specific item can talk with others to locate it at an affordable price. However, exact requirements come in handy for those situations when people want to dump their unwanted, worn-out furniture onto the library; the library then has ample grounds for not accepting the donation.

POLICIES AND PROCEDURES

Especially when library space is at a premium, clear policies and procedures about the use of the library are needed Maintenance is crucial because good upkeep prolongs the life of the library and its furniture. Eternal vigilance, and handy cleaning products, prevent unwanted carry-ins (food, drink, confetti) and take care of accidents.

Outside groups offer potential support for the library, so they should be encouraged to use the facility when it doesn't conflict with normal operations. A simple written agreement clarifies the library's position and the user group's responsibilities and indicates that the library is professional and businesslike. Users should have insurance, give a damage deposit, be responsible for setup and cleanup, and uphold all library regulations. They may also be able to pay a usage fee.

Careful scheduling guards against multiple groups using the library simultaneously. Although the library should be inviting, people overload lowers the professional attention that the librarian can give, besides producing conflict over book demands and noise levels.

A well-organized and pleasant facility demonstrates the librarian's concern for the users. The library is, after all, a special space. The extra effort put into making the facility comfortable, accessible, and manageable increases staff and user productivity and is a significant part of overall planning.

3

Material Resources

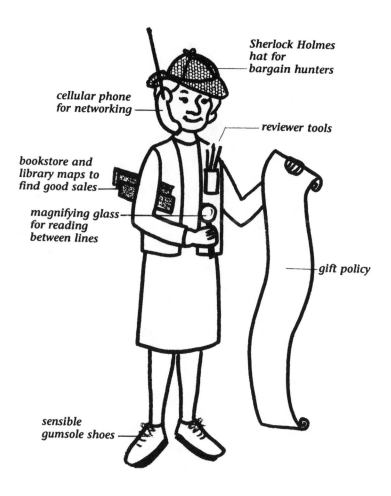

Sherlock Holmes
hat for
bargain hunters

cellular phone
for networking

reviewer tools

bookstore and
library maps to
find good sales

magnifying glass
for reading
between lines

gift policy

sensible
gumsole shoes

The heart of the library is its collection. And the collection is vulnerable when it comes to budget cutting. Too often governing boards do not realize the informational needs that libraries must address. There may be the general perception that people can give their books to the library and that that will suffice. Decisionmakers also forget the time and supply cost of processing materials. Even without a budget, librarians are usually expected to somehow continue developing the collection.

POLICIES

The first step in effective collection development is to educate key library players about the importance of high-quality collection development. A collection-development policy and procedures guide should be in place. Such a guide is paramount because it provides the basis for selection. It needs to include

- a basic selection philosophy, which is tied into the mission statement;
- criteria for selection for all media;
- procedures for challenged materials;
- criteria for withdrawing materials; and
- policies related to accepting gifts and donations.

A statement about present acquisition priorities may also be helpful. This might include points such as buying only paperbacks, single copies, or curricula-centered information books. Make these guidelines available for decisionmakers to peruse so that they are equally clear about professional collection principles.

DO LOOK A GIFT HORSE
IN THE MOUTH

Particularly in hard times, librarians are apt to accept everything that people donate. They figure that they can sift the chaff from the wheat. Such blind acceptance of donations can be a two-edged sword for several reasons. The library gains the reputation of a dumping ground for unwanted property, including outdated mildewed books. The time required to sort materials and find spaces for precious little memorabilia can be counterproductive to effective collection development. Persons who agree to donate their magazines or newspapers, once they're read, sometimes forget. Inevitably, those missing issues are the most highly sought after. (On a positive note, if a source can donate expensive periodicals such as the *Wall Street Journal* on a dependable schedule, the savings—and service—are great.)

Unless clear policies about accepting gifts and donations are communicated to donors, misunderstanding can arise when those prized old magazines fail to appear on the shelves or when the librarian omits a price value on in-kind contributions. The same criteria for selection should apply to purchased and donated works. Most librarians are not trained in appraising the market value of books, especially old ones; letters for tax purposes should stick to number of items received and not include estimates of their value.

On the plus side, libraries can introduce exciting donation programs, for example, birthday or adopt-a-book fund-raisers. Graduating students can clean their closets and donate high-demand curriculum-based or leisure books; graduating classes can give the library money for books as a valuable class gift.

The key to successful collection development is control of acquisitions by the librarian. (A wish list should always be on hand in case of sudden windfalls.) Public-relations techniques to take advantage of these options are covered in chapter 7.

PREVIEWING

Some librarians have to look at a book or nonprint item before they buy it. They have a point; reviews can be misleading (especially if written by the author's colleagues), and nothing beats looking at the real thing. However, that is no reason to pay full price for a book at a bookstore.

First, librarians can use bookstores as preview centers, jotting down titles as they scan volumes in succession and later finding cheaper places to buy those same volumes. Don't feel guilty! Not every perfume sprayed at store counters nor every pair of pants tried on in fitting rooms is bought. Bookstores know that libraries are prime markets, and that people who frequent libraries often buy books that they see and like. In a way, libraries are free publicity for publishers and bookstores.

Second, librarians can use other libraries as preview centers. Especially when immediacy is not an issue, librarians from financially strapped libraries can use more affluent libraries as models of collection development. Staff in those stocked libraries — whose high-demand titles are sometimes depleted — will be happy to know that librarians from poorer libraries are seeking to improve their own collections, thus lifting the burden on the more well-endowed libraries.

In larger library systems, a preview collection facilitates acquisitions. These centers are usually open to out-of-system librarians. By visiting these centers, librarians from less affluent libraries not only examine new resources but have the opportunity to network professionally with their counterparts and establish long-term relationships with other librarians.

Regional professional library organizations also provide previewing and reviewing opportunities. Usually one member serves as the clearinghouse and brings complementary copies of books to organization meetings. Attendees view the books, and each reviews a few books. At the next meeting those reviews are shared, and the reviewers keep the books. In this way, librarians know the reviewers personally and can usually trust their judgment.

ALTERNATIVE SOURCES

There is little reason ever to pay full price for library materials, especially books, when so many other alternatives exist. Keeping in mind high standards for acquisitions, librarians can find good values on needed materials. Here is a sampling of the variety of alternative suppliers.

When new editions arrive, well-endowed libraries often give their outdated copies to other libraries. Get on their list! If a well-stocked library weeds regularly and thoroughly, its castoffs may satisfy other libraries' needs.

Because most bookstores need the latest BIP (*Books in Print*), they get rid of their old copy: Be there to retrieve it. They also give discounts to libraries, depending on the number of books purchased within a given time frame. Bookstores often carry sections of bargain books or remainders. These are books that the publishers printed more copies of than they could sell easily and so they have wholesaled copies at ridiculously low prices to get rid of the inventory. These books may have bargain prices but must be scrutinized carefully for their usefulness, their currency, and their quality. Bookstores are also a good source of reference books in paperback, which are often excellent buys. Many of these titles are last year's editions of standard reference tools now issued in paperback but may have a good deal of value left.

Used bookstores can be a librarian's best friend. Not only can librarians get good buys but they can sell withdrawn materials to the bookstore owner (who usually gives a better trade-in through book credit rather than cash). These owners put items aside that they know the librarian wants, especially when a long-term business relationship has been developed. In one case, when a librarian was trying to develop the computer-books section through a grant and needed gifts in kind to demonstrate local support, the used-book dealer let her have all his stock of computer books free.

Wholesalers usually sell their books at 40 percent discounts. Check them out and avoid the retail bookstore. For instance, Ingram (P.O. Box 3006, La Vergne, TN 37086-1986) and Midwest Library Service (11443 St. Charles, Rock Rd., Bridgeton, MO 63014) provide dependable service. Look seriously at paperback distributors: Once one hardback copy is bought, paperback versions make good duplicates, especially if they are reinforced with plastic covers. Even general discount stores sometimes sell books.

Newsstands throw away old magazines when the new issues arrive; depending on their agreement with their distributors, they will give those copies to libraries.

Although the post office usually cannot give away undelivered mail, if magazine labels come off the covers, sometimes carriers can give those issues to libraries.

Books displayed at library conferences sell for good discounts, especially the last day of the conferences. Some exhibitors even give away their books to avoid having to cart them away.

Eager to recruit new business, organizations may offer free copies of their publications to libraries. Apply the same criteria for selection as for other purchases. These organizations sometimes represent the minority view; by acquiring these publications gratis, librarians can balance their collections more effectively.

Contact local representatives about government publications. Often, substantial volumes are available free upon request from government representatives. A quarterly pamphlet of low-cost and free materials is available from the Government Printing Office (Consumer Information Center, P.O. Box 100, Pueblo, CO 81002). The U.S. State Department Bureau of Public Affairs has free *Background Notes* about different countries. Government bodies also send promotional materials about their area upon request. Make use of taxpayer dollars.

Many companies and business organizations such as chambers of commerce provide free annual reports and consumer publications, for example *Aramco World*. Note, however, that these in-house publications usually have a definite bias; it is better to have bare shelves than huge quantities of misleading or inaccurate information. Price Waterhouse (1251 Avenue of the Americas, New York, NY 10020) has a fine series of booklets, available free upon request, on doing business abroad. Each booklet covers one country and is updated regularly. Librarians should take care to use strict guidelines for selecting and retaining free or bargain materials. It is extremely easy to fill up shelves—even warehouses—with freebies, but whether those materials are of value to students, teachers, and the curricular mission served by the library is quite another matter.

Remainder trade books are often greatly discounted by book distributors. Others offer good prices on used books. Representative services include

- Barnes & Noble, 126 Fifth Ave., New York, NY 10011

- Better Books Co., P.O. Box 9770, Fort Worth, TX 76107

- Econo-Clad Books, 2101 N. Topeka, Topeka KS 66606

- Edward R. Hamilton, Falls Village, CT 06031-5000

- Hotho & Co., P.O. Box 9738, Fort Worth, TX 76147-2738

- Permabound, Hertzberg-New Method, East Vandalia Rd., Jacksonville, IL 62650

- Publishers' Central Bureau, 1 Champion Ave., Avenel, NJ 07131

- Strand Book Store, 828 Broadway, New York, NY 10003

- Tartan Books Sales, 500 Arch St., Williamsport, PA 17705

- University Book Service, 2436 W. Granville Rd., Worthington, OH 43085

Book clubs usually provide great introductory offers and make their profits from long-term agreements. Often their best feature is their book annotations, which can be used in library promotions and for review purposes. Probably the best deal is to satisfy the original agreement in the lengthiest time and then drop the service. Some librarians default on the basic club agreement, but that is a shabby practice.

Publishers of library sciences books are on the lookout for insightful book reviewers. In most cases, those books or nonprint materials are free for the reviewing and can be added directly to the library. Look for requests for subject-specific reviewers and respond with a strong cover letter and high-quality sample reviews (even if they have never been published).

Sometimes outside vendors will give libraries commissions or books in reimbursement for allowing them to sell their wares at book fairs in the library, where the vendors have the advantage of meeting responsive consumers. Get the best agreement possible.

On a more idealistic plane, reading promotionals motivate students to read and to obtain books for themselves. Reading is Fundamental (Smithsonian Institution, 600 Maryland Ave. SW, Suite 500, Washington, D.C. 20560) is a national not-for-profit program heavily funded by the federal government. Librarians, or other program coordinators, develop a booklist from which students can choose books for themselves. The local institution pays about one-quarter of the cost, which is sometimes picked up by local businesses or library-friends groups.

Magazine distributors sometimes have a special program whereby local businesses can donate money for magazine subscriptions in return for magazine-cover publicity. Make sure to clear the ethical arrangement of such a partnership before pursuing this avenue. Some schools have regulations against solicitations even as passive as magazine covers.

Discount magazine subscription services are usually geared to educators and students. Their offerings are limited, so librarians usually have to use multiple magazine distributors to cover all needed titles. However, if the hassles of multiple renewal times are minimal, these suppliers can be cost-effective.

Troll and Scholastic are two reputable book-club distributors who sell high-quality books at reasonable prices. With quantity purchases, their brokers accrue points toward books and supplies. Elementary libraries especially take on this responsibility so that they can get the books they need. As with other sales promotions, promoting these commercial enterprises involves ethical ramifications that need to be carefully weighed.

Magazines and encyclopedia distributors enable libraries to acquire needed titles based on their endorsement of products being sold. Librarians need to look closely at their professional roles in encouraging users to buy these products.

Several periodicals list free or low-cost items for libraries. Representative titles and publishers include

- Educational Material Clearinghouse, School and Library Service, 1359 Michigami Dr., Cheboygan, MI 49721

- Educators Progress Series, 214 Center St., Randolph, WI 53956-9989

- *Free Materials for Schools and Libraries*, Box C34069, Seattle, WA 98124-1069

- Modern Talking Picture Service, 5000 Parks St. N., St. Petersburg, FL 33709

- *Public Information Materials*, Public Information Department, Federal Reserve Bank of New York, 33 Liberty St., New York, NY 10045

- *Vertical File Index*, H. W. Wilson, 950 University Ave., Bronx, NY 10452

Several book and periodicals exchange programs exist to provide missing copies of magazines or to distribute duplicative copies of books. These exchanges may be informal within regional library organizations or may extend to national and international efforts. The Duplicates Exchange Union (ALA, 50 E. Huron St., Chicago, IL 60611) is a voluntary, not-for-profit network of libraries that exchange periodicals, books, and other library materials. Items are available on a first-come basis. The Library of Congress, Exchange and Gift Division, gives away duplicate copies of books. Selection must be done on site, so libraries must write a letter of introduction and permission for a person in the Washington, D.C., area to choose materials. Franked labels for shipping books are available upon request from the local congressperson.

SUPPLIES

A certain advantage exists in having a low budget: Less time has to be devoted to processing materials. Also, less money has to be spent on supplies. However, there are innovative ways to find or create supplies.

As with buying library collections and furniture, acquiring supplies requires thoughtful comparative shopping. Those same sources that offer inexpensive equipment or books often provide supplies as well: industrial suppliers, bankrupt businesses, community agencies, warehouse distributors. Haunt the school lockers at the end of the year for writing instruments, paper, binders, notebooks, and great potential cleaning cloths.

Library supplies can also be created from recycled products. Used catalog cards were probably the first items recycled in libraries. "New" catalog cards can be typed on the clean side of old cards. Collect old card sets as library instructional aids. Use old cards as bookmarks and scratch paper. Glue three edges of cards to create book pockets. If desperate, use the clean side as a checkout card. Make sure to cross out the used side to prevent confusion to users or staff.

Recycled paper is ecological *and* cost-effective. Use the clean side of printer or copier paper in the original machine used. (Heavily inked paper does not work well in laser printers.) Cut up paper to use as scratch paper for notes. Write on the clean of used colored paper for flyers; tack the clean side onto a bulletin board for an attractive background.

Old newspapers make a good cover "cloth" for student artwork. Transform them into textbook covers. Use the Sunday comics as wrapping paper or display background. Crumple them up to create shipment packing material. In a real pinch, use them as newsprint. Of course, crumpled newspaper is great for wiping windows washed with an ammonia-water solution.

Large manilla envelopes serve several purposes. Reuse them for their original intent: mailing. File vertical-file materials, pictures, display elements, and other documents in them instead of using file folders (loose items stay better in envelopes anyway). Keep large envelopes by the circulation desk so that users can place borrowed materials in them, especially in bad weather.

Some magazines arrive in clear plastic bags. Make pencil-proof clear cases for signs. Send library materials home in them to protect items against rain and snow. Enclose book-cassette kits in them for easy access.

Old magazines are priceless. Clip significant articles for vertical files; *National Geographic* magazine is especially good. Clip illustrations for displays. Give an old book a face-lift with an appropriate picture, covering it with a clear vinyl adhesive sheet or varnish. Wrap gifts in attractive color spreads. One library made a unique wall covering from old *New Yorker* covers. Keep a box of withdrawn magazines for users to cut; it saves on the newer issues. Sell duplicate copies of magazines; users appreciate having a personal copy to clip at leisure.

Wallpaper samples make lively display backgrounds or lettering. Fold wallpaper into book jackets. Cover containers with samples.

Labels rejected by other offices find their use in libraries. Cover old vertical-file labels with them. Cut them into spine labels.

Clear vinyl adhesive sheets cover paperbacks easily and prolong their use. Sheets cover important signs and protect them against tears and marks. Use the sheets as an alternative to laminating. A good source for these sheets is Plastic Window Products Co., 3104 Skokie Valley Rd., Highland Park, IL 60035-1057.

Regardless of the state of the budget, librarians still need to address collection-development needs. This requires careful selection policies, creative searching for alternative suppliers and resource sharers, and thorough maintenance procedures.

Keeping resources in good shape is critical. Materials may need mending more often as fewer replacements can be purchased. Staff need to spot repair needs immediately so that materials can be fixed before they get worse. A wise preventative practice is to reinforce covers while processing them for the first time.

Assiduous weeding must also continue. A good-looking collection with fewer items will be used more often that a shoddy collection stuffed with outdated material. Besides, a well-weeded collection demonstrates careful selection and highlights subject gaps more quickly, resulting in donors being more apt to contribute toward the library's well-being.

NETWORKING

No library can serve as a completely self-sustaining operation in terms of resources — nor should it try. Tight finances and expanded service demands bring up the broader issue of information distribution. Libraries are beginning to be considered in terms of information *access* rather than information *housing*. Does it matter if the library does not own the hard copy of a periodical if its computer modem can download the full text? Some libraries have licenses to download cable broadcasts. (CNN offers a free agreement, so cost need not be an issue.) Libraries share special roving collections.

Probably the greatest benefit of networking among libraries is resource sharing. Coordinating resources has become a feasible way to magically expand library collections. For example, each librarian can subscribe to a different professional journal and pass it on, round-robin style, to the next library. (This method works best in a close-knit, small geographically contained network.) As librarians note possible purchases in the journals, they can share their collection-development intentions.

Union periodicals lists facilitate interlibrary loans and help librarians decide which magazines to subscribe to or drop. (Communication among librarians is crucial to prevent all union-list participants from dropping the same title!) Union index lists facilitate special research projects. Only one library in a network needs to buy *Library Literature*, for instance.

Centralized collections, for example of audiovisual materials, provide access to expensive materials at a low per-cost basis. Each library can collect bibliographies and other access tools on a specialized topic, such as ethnic studies, acting as a clearinghouse for information about collection development in that area. Each library can develop strong holdings in one area, such as poetry or science. Other libraries can borrow those books when needed for specialized research rather than buying little-used volumes. A union list of those special collections facilitates this collection-development practice. Libraries can borrow whole sections from each other, such as Shakespeare materials, when high-demand books for a class project are all in circulation. (Invariably, everyone studies Native Americans simultaneously.)

As curriculum needs change, books from one library can be lent or given to another library. In one case, a librarian was weeding materials from the 1960s; a librarian from another school created a special Sixties Primary Sources collection with these materials because the history department covered this period in depth. When another school studies that period, this now site-independent collection can be loaned to it upon request. One library's weeded collection may fit the bill for another library.

Coordinated efforts also result in cost-effective purchasing. Publishers and suppliers often give discounts on multiple copies of books and joint purchases of equipment or subscription services. Procedures for purchase orders and reimbursements should be developed by the network and cleared by appropriate administrators to ensure worry-free acquisitions.

Networking facilitates processing of new acquisitions. Particularly if books are purchased jointly, central processing can be done when the materials arrive. The cost of this convenience is standardization. Libraries can ill afford the luxury and inefficiency of highly individualized card catalogs. They must agree on classification policies. Especially as libraries increase interlibrary loaning, their users need the security that they will find needed information in the same classification area, regardless of where the item is usually stored.

A POINT OF ETHICS

When developing collections librarians can slip into murky ethical waters. The chief conflict is balancing the very real needs of users and the rights of producers and suppliers. Before sinking into an ethical quagmire, librarians should have a clear ethical stance and be able to justify their decisions.

Reviewing is a fruitful way to acquire library materials gratis. However, some publishers, especially of videotapes, caution reviewers not to add these items to libraries because that means one less copy of the product will sell. If reviewers really like the materials, they should purchase a copy for their libraries.

Group purchases of reference books, especially, can entice school librarians to participate in sales to parents. Knowing that 10 sales result in a free copy of a standard encyclopedia set can be a powerful enducement. Librarians, however, are not supposed to encourage specific products. Rather, they are supposed to provide objective criteria upon which users can decide what resources should be purchased. The stakes are high, but it would be more ethical for a librarian to quit her job and become a full-time salesperson rather than advocate a certain product while holding a professional position.

Computer software and videotapes can be extremely easy and cheap to duplicate. Photocopy costs usually outstrip the cost of buying another copy of a book, but these other media tempt librarians to ignore copyright for the sake of the users. This issue is clearer because most such products note legal copying practice. Not only are librarians legally liable for transgressing copyright laws, but they also serve as unprofessional and unethical models for their users.

Videotapes, even when not duplicated, can pose legal problems. Some libraries borrow tapes from other libraries or rent them from videotape outlets. In most cases, librarians are not legally allowed to show them as separate programs for the public without proper permission from the producers or distributors. A safer, though usually more expensive approach, is to join a regional AV cooperative that has licensing rights to duplicate materials.

Telecommunications poses real ethical issues, and the legalities are still being ironed out. Enough public-domain electronic bulletin boards exist so that librarians should not have to resort to illegal access to telecommunications services. Unethical activity becomes more tempting when on-line databases are used; does the library have the right to download a big chunk of citations and then create subcategories off-line? Usually not.

When about CD-ROM and microform subscription services? Some of them do not require the subscriber to return the older version of their product. As a result, some libraries give their older version to a poorer library. Rather than risk possible wrath from the supplier, librarians should ask permission before sharing.

A grayer ethical area exists relative to suppliers' premiums: those little promotional gifts that publishers and distributors give to steady and prospective customers. How many librarians collect posters and supplies at conferences? Although such loading up is business as usual, the ethics behind this behavior may be questionable. Those freebies get calculated into higher costs to consumers and are daily publicity for the companies. Those extra-friendly salesfolk remain in the memory when purchasing time eventually comes around. The safest ethical route to take is to pay for those tokens. But it takes a strong sense of principle, especially for the budget-beleagured librarian.

Another gray area is discount buying. Some financially constrained libraries buy books at large discounts (say, 40 percent) and resell them to users at face value. Bookstores have no problem with this; some librarians may. The main question is whether the library wants to get into the bookstore business. Unless the library already deals with textbooks, the best approach is to avoid this possible conflict of interest.

4

Computer-Related Issues

satellite dish
to get all
technology channels

calculator
for best buys

floppy disks for
freeware and
public domain
software

computer glossary

surge-protect
power strips to
handle surges
in acquisitions

track shoes to
keep up with
technology
and to jump
financial hurdles

For those libraries lacking a telephone connection, the idea of purchasing computers may seem unrealistic. However, the demand for computers in the library runs high, and this demand can be used as leverage when asking for a budget raise. Although computers may not make life easier, they offer new, substantial possibilities for processing and accessing information.

GROUNDWORK

While waiting for the money and equipment to roll in, librarians should use this time to learn more about computer technology, from their present level of competence to the next level. Several aspects of computer technology deserve attention:

- hardware and software trends;

- library applications;

- software use;

- systems analysis (putting equipment together);

- costs;

- means of acquiring computer-related resources.

Librarians can gather information from library literature, professional meetings, continuing-education courses, and working with colleagues. By keeping current, librarians have a better idea of what is available and can act quickly if a financial window of opportunity appears. Knowledgeable librarians also have higher credibility, can help others with computer issues, and are more apt to get the computer materials needed.

Librarians should also examine the present situation of the library and the environment in which it operates in terms of its relationship to computer technology. How will space be affected? Is space adequate for all computer-related needs? Will furniture need to be rearranged? How do computers affect traffic and noise patterns?

Is the site environmentally prepared? Do enough outlets exist in the right places? How old is the wiring? If cables will be installed, are ducts available? Are humidity and temperature appropriate? Can a telephone line be connected for telecommunications needs? Is the area safe from hazards?

How prepared are staff members? What training do they need ahead of time? Do they need to feel more comfortable psychologically about the advent of computer technology?

What is the role of computer technology within the larger organization? Are key decisionmakers supportive of computers?

The more librarians can prepare the site and the people involved, the easier will be the transition to computer use.

PLANNING AHEAD

The most effective way to incorporate computer technology into the library is to plan for it. Even if no machine is in sight for the next five years, developing a plan of action helps sensitize decisionmakers to library needs.

Because the library's governing body may control what computer hardware is acquired, the librarian would do well to concentrate on the *functions* that the computer can perform in support of library goals. In that way the library can take advantage of possible batch purchases without being tied prematurely to one system platform. Some typical library functions that lend themselves to computer incorporation include

- budgeting;

- record-keeping;

- cataloging;

- managing circulation (and overdues);

- providing bibliographic services;

- maintaining address and phone lists of Friends of the library and donors;

- reporting and publishing;

- instructing users in accessing information.

Whatever the function, the librarian should include the following elements in the detailed plan:

- summary of current practice;

- information and data used;

- how information and data are processed;

- who sends and who receives the information and data;

- current costs and benefits (both tangibles and intangibles);

- alternatives to present practice and relative costs and benefits;

- evaluation of present and alternative solutions.

The next step in planning is to consider strategies for getting the computer technology needed. Use logic to demonstrate to decisionmakers the cost-effectiveness of computer technology. Show different ways to find funding for technology. Use competition to show how comparable libraries use computer technology, emphasizing the need to give equally good service. If local libraries use little technology, find model libraries with successful computer experience and appeal to decisionmakers' desires to be the best. It may be helpful to provide computer access for key decisionmakers. Ensure that decisionmakers and others have computer access. The best way to convince people is to let them convince themselves. If they have a good experience with a computer, they'll be more likely to support computer acquisitions. Dealers may rent a system to the library for a trial period. Individual dealers may demonstrate their goods at the library, or a group of dealers may participate in a library computer fair for the public.

Build in stages. Start with one function or one computer system and demonstrate a long-term game plan for effective computer incorporation. Make it easy for decisionmakers to say yes by minimizing the costs and modifications necessary. Make payment plans workable.

Think globally. No best time exists for computer purchasing; the development curve hasn't peaked yet. A significant capital campaign may be easier to mount than a small-scale effort, and a fully integrated system that satisfies a range of functions may have greater donor appeal.

By developing a repertoire of possible options, the librarian can fit the approach to the context of the total system in which the library operates. For example, the administrator who has little technological background and thinks of computers in terms of outrageous utility bills will require more hand holding and subtle convincing on a personal level. A can-do decisionmaker might be approached with a major capital-campaign plan. Much more is at stake than computer technology: Political savvy is required.

ACQUISITIONS

Because computer technology is usually a big-bill item, librarians need to know exactly what they want, and then how to choose the right supplier. A good analogy is buying a car: Be thoroughly prepared!

Once a feasibility plan has been approved, a detailed list of hardware and software must be drawn up with every possible specification included:

- dimensions;

- memory (RAM and ROM);

- operating system;

- monitor: type of color, interface, touch-screen or not;

- keyboard: layout, function keys, attached or movable;

- peripheral storage: external disk drives, hard drives, backup devices;

- external input devices: mouse, joystick, paddle, writing screen;

- telecommunications: interface, modem;

- modifications for disabled persons: voice command, alternative pads, etc.;

- printers: interface, quality, speed, ink quality;

- expandability;

- compatibility within and between brands;

- ease of operation;

- documentation: content, readability, completeness;

- delivery and installation: time frame, site preparation;

- training: content, delivery system (lecture, video, computer), time frame;

- servicing and warranties: on-site or not, base costs, turn-around time, replacements, backup equipment;

- upgrades: cost, ease.

Librarians should examine different types of operating systems (e.g., MS-DOS [IBM] vs. ProDOS [Apple]) and different models within a computer family (e.g., Mac Classic vs. LC), prioritizing the specifications listed. For portable computers, compatibility with other hardware used within the larger organization is not so critical.

But compatibility should be considered if for no other reason than that computer problems do arise, and technical help or a spare machine is sometimes needed.

Once the specifications are clarified and potential computer items are in mind, then it is time for comparison shopping. In some cases, the librarian calls for bids; in other cases, the librarian is free to choose any supplier. In either case, thorough planning and incisive, assertive questioning are keys to successful, if stressful, buying. One final note: Take the time necessary to make a rational decision. Prices are falling and new models are coming out; no all-time-great offer exists. It is a buyer's market.

SUPPLIERS

With the large discounts now available for computer-related products, full-price purchasing has become virtually unnecessary. Opportunities for getting more bang for the buck abound. Take advantage of educational discounts available for educators and students of higher learning through school districts, institutes of higher learning, and even directly from suppliers. Visit retail computer stores and try all the equipment. Bargain thoroughly but don't feel committed to buying there. Usually a better deal exists elsewhere. Try warehouse stores and computer superstores such as Price Club and CompUSA. Because of high-volume business, they offer very competitive prices and replace defective equipment.

Mail-order businesses are increasing in number and reliability. They can offer enticing deals, especially with packaged offers (combined hardware and software). Check with other librarians to find out how dependable these sources are. It is usually safer to buy only well-known products from these companies. Four reputable suppliers are

- Dell Computer: (800) 426-5150;

- Gateway 2000: (800) 523-2000;

- Northgate Computer Systems: (800) 548-9016;

- Zeos International: (800) 423-5891.[1]

Used-computer stores vary widely in quality. The jury is out about the relative cost savings. Some say that discounts on new machines, especially on closeouts as new models come in, equal used-computer prices; others feel used machines can be financially worthwhile. Machinery over five years old probably isn't very useful. Any used machine, like a used car, needs careful inspection. The dealer needs to be reputable — and available if problems arise.

Very knowledgeable computer buyers find good prices at computer swap shows. The fair atmosphere attracts a certain breed of computer groupie. Just eavesdropping on the conversations can be fascinating. With careful comparision buying, librarians have been known to buy a computer system piece by piece, assembling it at the library. But you have to know what you are doing! Remember, swap meets are not known for good follow-up services or solid warranties.

Conferences are more formal gatherings for computer-technology exhibits. Dealers give discounts on site and via order forms to complete back in the library.

Users and user groups offer lots of advice on suppliers and programs, based on personal experience. Some community-spirited groups enter into partnerships with local agencies, providing them with free computers and technical assistance. Word of mouth seems to be particularly useful to find out what is happening in growing industries such as computer technology.

Explore resource sharing. Join with other libraries or like institutions to take advantage of group purchasing rates. Although sharing computers is usually counterproductive (the computer is never available when it is needed), CD-ROM-based retrospective conversion products may be shared among librarians if properly licensed for the group.

Adventurous libraries can serve as demonstration or pilot sites for computer technology. Producers test their products in progress before marketing them. Although prices may be very attractive, test centers take a big risk: Computer technology may have serious defects that can damage existing library data.

SOFTWARE

Software can be another strain on the library budget. Librarians must carefully balance high-cost programs that specifically address a library function and low-cost generic programs. They must also compare expensive, powerful programs with lower-performance public-domain programs. The underlying issue is one of adaptability versus standards. The more creative and knowledgeable the librarian, the more options are available.

Several questions should guide software choices. First, do software programs meet basic criteria of accurate content, technical correctness, clean visuals, ease of use, and adequate documentation? Poorly written software is expensive in the long run, no matter how attractive the cover price. Second, how much power should the software possess? Smaller libraries usually do not exploit the power features of high-end products, nor need they. Third, what kind of software do related libraries or organizational entities use? Sometimes software can be copied throughout a system, depending on the software agreement. If the same data are used throughout a system, be they book titles or user names, programs that can transfer data increase productivity for all parties. Finally, what level of competencies do program users need to have? Some low-cost programs include little documentation; they may use standard protocols that experienced software users may know intuitively but neophytes will find frustrating without clearly written support.

A good low-cost integrated program can satisfy most library needs. Products such as Microsoft Works, PFS: First Choice, and AppleWorks combine word processing, database management, spreadsheets, and telecommunications. Files can be transferred from one application to another to facilitate compiling reports and other documents. These products are simple to use and employ a consistent command structure, so aides can be taught how to use them as well. Particularly as librarians take advantage of library templates, many library functions can be carried out satisfactorily with these simple systems:

- word processing: forms, reports, publicity, labels;

- database management: bibliographies, AV files, ordering, basic cataloging, simple circulation;

- spreadsheets: budgets, circulation records, statistics, collection analysis.

Public-domain products provide low-cost alternatives for basic types of programs. These programs are usually written by public-minded folks who believe in computers "for the people." Freeware is copyrighted but distributed in much the same way as are public-domain programs. For shareware programs the author asks for a small fee if the user keeps the copyrighted product; some programs can be copied freely (freeware). Unfortunately, some of these well-meaning programmers are not sophisticated developers; programs may be very limited or bug-ridden. The best insurance for getting satisfactory software is to keep current on computer software reviews and acquire software from reputable sources to prevent getting computer viruses. For instance, FredWriter and PC-Write are satisfactory word-processing programs; ProComm and Red Ryder are easy-to-use telecommunications interface programs. Representative software suppliers include

- The Public Domain Exchange, 2074C Walsh Ave., Dept. 680, Santa Clara, CA 95050;

- Reasonable Solutions, 2101 W. Main St., Medford, OR 97501;

- California Freeware, 1747 E. Ave. Q, #C-1, Palmdale, CA 93550.

TELECOMMUNICATIONS

Telecommunications, basically a computer connected to a phone line, represents the library's information link with the world. Even libraries with limited budgets (and a modem and telephone) can provide valuable telecommunications services by using public-domain interface software and public-access or low-cost electronic-database services.

Computer bulletin boards work like their corkboard counterparts, providing information on a variety of topics; electronics-based interest groups abound. Users can access by subject or input their own comments. These electronic bulletin-board systems (BBS) are often free except for telephone connection time. Check local computer publications and user groups for possible numbers. Note that BBSs vary widely in quality, so use them with discretion and be careful about the computer viruses that can be downloaded into your computer.

Electronic mail services concentrate on transferring messages between service participants. These services overlap BBSs in that messages can be sent to all members; the advantage of E-mail is that information can be sent selectively. An increasing number of state and regional library and educational networks offer free-access services. Typical menu items include conferences, reviews, news updates, and announcements.

On-line databases comprise the bulk of telecommunications services. Usually commercial enterprises index publications and create search protocols to facilitate information retrieval. However, some universities offer free access to their on-line catalogs, which helps libraries with limited budgets get materials through interlibrary loan (ILL). Some major commercial database services, such as Prodigy and Dialog, offer low-cost services for home or educational use; these services typically contain a limited number of the service's total database repertoire. Off-hour access also lowers database access cost. Trial periods to test database services may be low-cost or free as inducement to join. If users and decisionmakers are enthusiastic enough about their use, they may find the needed money to support such database access.

PUTTING THE LIBRARY INTO GOOD FORM USING TEMPLATES

Is the same library data used in a variety of ways? Do reports about the items serve different purposes and need the attention of different people? Information might include a computer-software inventory, a periodicals list, specialized bibliographies, a donor or volunteer list, even an order form. These data are perfect candidates for database management.

Database computer programs provide powerful help. Fields are used to organize data and to facilitate searching for items that match specific criteria. Such programs sort items by these different fields and take advantage of secondary sorts to provide additional structure. Data can be easily updated by changing only those records, for example unfilled orders, that need changing. Software generates different kinds of reports, using only those fields that apply to the particular use and user.

To make the best use of databases, and to save money by using one utility program rather than a number of limited one-function library software programs, use templates to manipulate data efficiently. The sequence, field name, and general layout can clarify databases and reports.

Templates need not be created from scratch: Template exchange clearinghouses for librarians exist for Apple, IBM, and Macintosh environments. Probably the most well-known center is the Apple Library Template Exchange (10281 Bandley Dr., Cupertino, CA 95014). Also, librarians can translate paper forms into machine format. In either case, critically evaluate these templates and forms. No perfect template exists, and local use may dictate customization. Additionally, by building on existing templates or forms, a librarian can achieve a better product.

There are several points to consider when designing a template or evaluating an existing one. What is the purpose of the information and database? Think of all the possible ways to manipulate the data. Plan for the future as much as possible: What expansion of the information is possible? How might the database be linked with other databases?

What kind of information should be included? Consider who uses the template and database.

What will be the field names or labels? Although names should be short to conserve space, they should be clear and meaningful. Avoid abbreviations. Include a couple of extra fields for future designation; it is very difficult to add fields later in some database programs.

Is the first field the most important or most-used field? In some programs, the first field may be searched faster than the others.

Are similar types of fields grouped together? For example, standard bibliographic information may be grouped in the same zone. For an acquisitions template, information about ordering and the supplier may belong together. It is useful to visually group like items together as well, drawing a line between zones or creating boxes around like fields.

Is the sequence of fields logical? Using the same order-form example, try starting with bibliographic data, then supplier information, then ordering history, then destination details.

Does the template look consistent — is spacing the same throughout? Are the lengths and widths of fields regularized so that three or fewer variations exist? Is typography the same, or at least varied according to some obvious rationale?

Is the template laid out visually such that if printed from the screen it would look esthetically pleasing? Are field names placed along one edge only or are they placed in a two-column format? Using one line for two fields shortens the form and adds pleasing variety. Notice that staggered fields require greater attention from the inputter: Right-hand fields may get skipped.

Does the template have a short, clear title? Could a new user understand its purpose?

Are clear instructions provided? Example records should be included. Any specific inputting requirements should be stated clearly, for example, date: month/day/year - ##/##/## - 3/15/92. Instructions should be tested for clarity and completeness by potential users.

Show the template design and instructions to people who will use the form. It is much easier to change a design before data are entered. Test the template using a small number of records to see how the data are manipulated and modify it if need be. Let the template give library functions the form to put information to work.

NOTE

[1]James Wils LaRue, "Shoppin' Around," *Wilson Library Bulletin* (April 1992): 88-89.

5

Human Resources

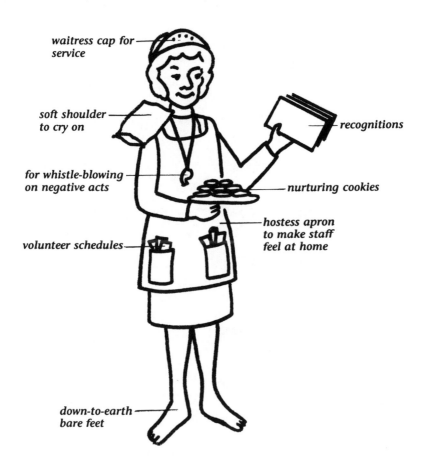

waitress cap for service

soft shoulder to cry on

recognitions

for whistle-blowing on negative acts

nurturing cookies

hostess apron to make staff feel at home

volunteer schedules

down-to-earth bare feet

The most valuable single resource in libraries is librarians; they provide a vital link between information and information seeker. As they develop means to attract and use others to support the library, they provide the foundation of financial stability for high-quality library service.

STAFFING

Often a limited budget necessitates reducing the number of valuable staff or staff time. Librarians may become beleaguered and actually less productive because of increased job stress. Librarians need to find volunteer help to fill the temporary gap. Staff are useful for daily operation, instruction and programs, development, and general support. As community members see the potential services in a well-staffed library, they are more likely to fund such positions. Note that volunteers cannot substitute for professional expertise; rather, they reflect and implement the professional's vision.

Although more and more families contain two breadwinners, several sources for volunteer library aides exist:

- library-school student (schools have requirements that supervisors have to meet, so check to make sure that the library is qualified);

- students (teenagers under 16 years old are especially good if well trained);

- parents, particularly those committed to good library service (both men and women);

- community members (businesses, volunteer groups, retirees).

Businesspeople and retired citizens can be particularly helpful. Many businesses include volunteer community service as part of their mission; those employees who use the library are good prospects because they have a personal commitment to effective library service. The other group, senior citizens, are experienced and usually can relate well to youngsters (check this out by personal reference).

With all these wonderful resources out there, why aren't they flocking to libraries? Because they have not been asked. It is as simple as that. That personal touch, telling people that they make a difference, is the key to successful recruitment. But how does one get to know a potential volunteer?

- through networking with librarians, library friends and users, and neighbors;

- by speaking at PTAs and local service clubs;

- by making announcements in publications (newspapers, in-house publications, community bulletins);

- by following leads from other persons;

- by talking to people who attend library events.

It is not surprising that the key to motivating potential volunteers is to appeal to each person's needs for status, for recreation, or for social activity. The title of library assistant or representing the library at service clubs can satisfy the need for status. Storytelling can be a welcome recreational activity. And working at the circulation desk or planning a library reception can satisfy the need for social activity. Volunteers may also wish simply to feel useful or to help their own children, learn skills, or better their employment opportunities. Reading to house-bound people and tutoring can make volunteers feel useful.

Learning computer skills or ways to create displays can broaden one's education. And a record of dependable work as a library volunteer can be an impressive addition to a resume.

Librarians should also think in terms of possible barriers that potential volunteers might face. And the more librarians can help individuals solve these problems, the more likely they will be able to recruit good people. Typical issues to address include negative past experiences, low self-esteem, lack of experience, fear of the unknown, logistics (transportation, babysitting, timing), and any language problems or barriers.

Motivated volunteers expect follow-through. They need to be interviewed in terms of their interests, abilities, and time commitments. Next, library functions should match their personal profiles; the job assignment should also take into consideration the volunteer's preference for one steady job or a variety of tasks. Only after clear expectations and performance standards are stated should they be trained.

A thorough and clear policy-and-procedure manual should guide the training so that volunteer staff can proceed in case experienced staff are absent. Other instructional aids include peer training, video lessons, and 3-by-5-inch reference cards. Ideally, the following steps should occur in training:

- The trainer explains and models the correct procedure.

- The trainer guides the trainee step by step in the specific procedure.

- The trainer supervises the trainee's actions and corrects actions as needed.

- The trainee carries out the process correctly and independently.

As a manager, the professional librarian needs to oversee scheduling, supervision (noting different person's needs for close or casual guidance), evaluation, and problem solving.

A mentality may exist that volunteers are second-rate, that they cannot be dependable or accountable. Neither is true. Volunteers need to know that their contributions are meaningful, and that their performance levels are important. A name tag with a library logo is one symbol of a significant contribution. Most people want to do their best and may need help in knowing how to improve their behavior. The sooner problems can be recognized and solved in cooperation with the volunteer, the more successful the experience will be for both parties.

Equally important is recognizing good work. Particularly when persons are not paid for their work, they need to know that they are valued, especially for specific tasks that are well done. A few ideas follow:

- Give at least token gifts for service: notepads, pins, certificates.

- Give library privileges: free photocopying, no-limit checkout privileges.

- Throw a party.

- Write a personal thank-you note or a good reference letter.

Volunteers not only give valuable service hours, they serve as supporters to get out the word in the community that the library deserves strong financial support.

INTEREST GROUPS

Interest groups represent specialized support for libraries. Particularly because libraries are involved in such a variety of activities, plenty of opportunity exists for building coalitions with interest groups to advance libraries.

Interest groups can be enlisted for several purposes. In fact, having a list of potential activities that interest groups can do provides these parties with immediate concrete actions that can make a difference in the library. This list also starts interest groups brainstorming about additional contributions they can make; the more interest groups feel a sense of ownership in helping the library, the more effective they become.

Probably the most often-cited function that interest groups accomplish is fund-raising and donating. Besides giving money and gifts in kind individually and as a group, interest groups can run fund-raising campaigns such as book fairs and telethons. Interest-group members can also help in staffing, either by donating their own time or by recruiting other people to volunteer their time. Based on the group's expertise, members can provide valuable service: repairing equipment, construction, duplicating publications, computer programming. Legal experts can help librarians develop policies. Those interest-group members who have good insights into library operations and the needs of users can give useful input for creating workable policies.

The most encompassing role that interest groups can play is that of library advocates and supporters. They can network with other people to broaden the support base.

Library interest groups comprise many different types of people. In some cases, a group may decide to use the library to advance its own causes. Typical groups fitting that description include book-discussion groups, computer-user groups, film aficionados, and story-telling guilds. In other cases, the library may call on outside groups such as landscaping enthusiasts, church groups, service clubs, or youth organizations. Or the library may establish an interest group based on library needs; this normally takes the form of a Friends of the Library program. Community members, students and other youth, parents, educators, and other librarians may all belong to library interest groups.

The relationship between libraries and interest groups is a delicate balance between autonomy and interdependence. Because interest groups are separate entities, librarians serve as coalition builders rather than as group administrators. Likewise, interest groups can recommend actions to take in the library, but they do not have the power to mandate change. The two groups are considered partners, planning jointly when mutually agreed-upon causes can be addressed more effectively by a broader-based constituency. Ideally, each partner should communicate regularly with the other about activities and joint plans. Some useful methods are regular meetings, newsletters, and bulletin boards (corkboard or electronic).

How do interest groups gear up for action? First, the group needs a clearly defined goal and a workable strategy to accomplish it. Ideally, a group should develop the plan together with the librarian to maximize positive results. In planning, the group and the librarian need to assess what resources, both material and human, are available. Additionally, they need to know what obstacles exist to counter success. Tasks should be divided into small, concrete steps with realistic deadlines. Next, they communicate their plan and goal publicly. Networking is imperative to garner broader support.

The group needs to achieve tangible results within a reasonable time and then publicize its success. Follow-up is also needed to provide continuity and to expand upon the foundation made by the group's efforts.

Interest groups do not follow one mode: Some are task-oriented, some emphasize public relations, and others are mainly social groups. All have legitimate roles as library supporters.

HUMAN NETWORKS

When budgets are constricted, librarians may feel frustrated and isolated. However, other librarians are likely to share the same predicament. Networking, then, becomes a natural and viable activity for mutual support and problem solving.

Although the term *networking* may conjure up visions of high-tech cables, it basically refers to any type of connection. Sharing ideas by mail may be a more effective form of networking than participating in a LAN (local area network).

Even with a zero budget, libraries can share in a network. An existing collection may be useful to others, and the materials borrowed from other libraries offset worries that any one collection will disappear. Networks can develop clearinghouses for library documents and databases. Expertise and experience are priceless — and worthy of sharing. Access to other people and institutions further broadens the network and makes it more useful to all.

A major benefit of networking is maximizing human resources. Although professional skills should not be abused, an occasional brief call for timely technical help saves frustration, effort, and, possibly, costly repairs. Librarians can share common concerns and issues. Particularly when librarians from different types of libraries meet, developments across professional and geographic lines are shared. Limited budgets often constrain time to visit other libraries; network meetings at different sites provide an opportunity to compare services and collections.

Potentially the greatest advantage of networking is human-resource development. Networking offers two distinct methods of training: Members within the network can train each other, or an outside consultant can train all the network members.

One simple way to facilitate training is to generate a needs-assessment and resources list: what librarians want to learn and what they can teach. As librarians meet regularly to network, they can conduct valuable workshops at no cost. When an outside person is needed, grant money or state funding may be found to underwrite this cooperative-based training.

On a broader scale, professional involvement in regional, state, and national organizations provides access to current library trends and trendsetters. These organizations' regular publications give thoughtful advice and note useful resources. Conferences offer state-of-the-art demonstrations and products. Committee membership allows librarians to exchange ideas and work on significant library issues. Contact with other librarians and agencies may lead to donations and opportunities. Moreover, such organizations carry professional and political clout, which can be used to justify library requests.

Even if librarians cannot afford to belong to several organizations, local networks offer a window for professional development. Members report on associations developments, and they pass on information gleaned from conferences and institutes. Furthermore, librarians can provide members with input to improve organization and services.

Although a network of like-minded librarians is the most logical type to join, networking can be considered a state of mind. Networks surround libraries daily. For example, educators and their associated professional networks provide information about resources in many fields. The training opportunities may lend themselves to library applications. Librarians can provide a broad interdisciplinary perspective on resources and curriculum development.

Parents, grandparents, and alumni link school libraries to the community and to local businesses. They may donate needed equipment and volunteer time. In turn, librarians can conduct workshops for parents on family literacy, computer technology, storytelling, and other skills.

Community businesses and agencies cosponsor events and underwrite special projects. Libraries can offer them display space for nonprofit purposes and opportunities to work with library users. Libraries can also offer collection and research help.

In each case, the network succeeds when the group's purpose is well defined, when equity between members is maintained, when membership is voluntary and when belonging makes a difference. Collections and services for each member should complement other participants. A fine line exists between cooperation and competition.

ADVOCACY IN ACTION

Communities have the power to save libraries. Here is just one example among many of libraries being valued by local citizens. The West Bridgewater (Massachusetts) Public Library was about to open when a financial shortfall threatened to close the doors even before the opening ceremony. The Friends of the Library organized, sending flyers to voters, coordinating a telethon, getting citizens out to town meetings. The library was saved.

Other local advocacy groups have been successful through

- writing letters to the editor;

- distributing library support buttons;

- donating facilities and materials;

- selling products to raise funds;

- making library repairs;

- holding "book-ins."[1]

Making their voices heard, supportive interest groups and network members can help libraries get the funding they need to serve their communities.

NOTE

[1]Marilyn Gardner, "Readers Become Noisy Advocates," *Christian Science Monitor*, 9 July 1991, 14.

6

Information Services

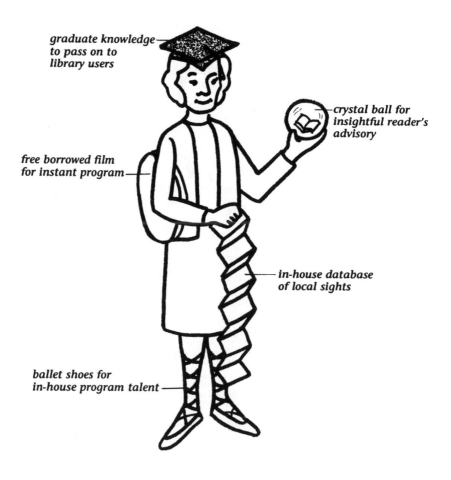

graduate knowledge to pass on to library users

crystal ball for insightful reader's advisory

free borrowed film for instant program

in-house database of local sights

ballet shoes for in-house program talent

Even without a budget, librarians can provide service. The time that would be used to acquire and process materials can be dedicated to processing information by retrieving, organizing, and sharing it. By taking advantage of lean times to build up information-service stockpiles, librarians will be able to cash in those chips for greater financial support when times become more prosperous.

RETRIEVING INFORMATION

At the most basic level, libraries exist to store and retrieve information for users. Even when budgets go down, requests for information remain steady or even go up. Therefore, librarians have to know their collections thoroughly in order to ferret out information needed by their users. In fact, budget-constrained librarians should increase efforts to provide personalized and more effective retrieval services.

Provide a high-quality readers' advisory. This service can assume various forms:

- theme- or reading-level-based binders of annotated bibliographies and book excerpts;

- annotated booklist bookmarks;

- topical displays and bulletin boards;

- computerized databases; and

- even reader's advice livened up in fortune-teller guise.

Offer selective dissemination of information. Prime users and interest groups fill out profile forms indicating topics of importance to them. As materials come in, subjects are matched with the profile, and the users are notified.

Develop referral systems to link users with other information centers. Especially as libraries become access points rather than self-contained warehouses, librarians should help users get information regardless of physical location. In this way, the community will regard librarians as necessary professional information brokers. The status of individual libraries is actually enhanced by a good referral service.

ORGANIZING INFORMATION

As professionals, librarians interact with information: selecting, evaluating, organizing, and synthesizing it. The final information package represents the professional's ability to bring order out of the chaos of dispersed data. A limited budget actually reveals the librarian's resourcefulness in providing information in a prepackaged usable form.

Aware librarians keep track of frequently asked questions and maintain "hot files" to organize and make available information about current topics of interest to users. These hot files represent efficient hours of researching and information gathering. They may be kept in used large manila envelopes; content is definitely more important than form. Typical hot files centralize information on school assignments, national issues, community concerns, and upcoming elections.

Packaging information can demonstrate librarian ingenuity — and insight on user needs. Some possibilities include

- study-skills packets: Classify pages from different documents into diagnostic tests and "tutorial" activities.

- "clipped notes": Create an attractive booklet on basic library skills.

- Research "survival kit": Package guidelines on research strategies and basic reference tools into a brochure or Hyper-Card format.

- self-help directories: Use library-created computer databases to generate publications on local educational and recreational opportunities.

- genre binders: Excerpt illustrations and texts to create mini-anthologies for browsing.

Local information represents a great opportunity for budget-limited librarians to show off their professional skill. Data about specific local resources are often dispersed widely; investigative librarians can gather data to create valuable in-house databases. Not only does the library fulfill its role as a true information center, it strengthens its support base by involving the community in its creation and use. Listings may take the form of index-card tickler files, resource-file directories, or computer databases. Content, which is based on user needs, may include

- employment leads;

- volunteer organizations;

- age-specific services;

- health care;

- educational offerings;

- personal help sources;

- recreational activities;

- speakers' bureaus;

- political groups;

- survival information.

INSTRUCTION

Instruction is another vital library service, whether as part of training or management, in the form of teaching information skills, or as a program piece (e.g., storytelling or readers theatre). For library-based instruction to be effective, several questions must be answered satisfactorily.

What is the purpose of the instruction? Especially with limited budgets, all efforts must focus on the library's mission statement. An assessment of user needs and available resources maximizes instructional effect. Typical aims are

- to provide intellectual access to information;

- to provide physical access to information, such as training on equipment;

- to train staff and volunteers in library operations;

- to provide learning activities that encourage lifelong reading, such as storytelling and readers theatre workshops.

What is the content of the instruction? Don't limit it to traditional library offerings. The library's unique instructional niche — informational skills — should be exploited, but this instructional base should also be expanded to include

- storytelling;

- selecting computer software;

- starting a business;

- computer care;

- film appreciation;

- cartooning;

- writing mysteries;

- geneology;

- English as a second language;

- oral history;

- collecting;

- interpretive dance; and

- architecture.

Each of these offerings deals with forms of information and ways to interact with them. Several of them involve local interest groups who can conduct the workshops. By involving others, the library broadens its instructional base and its overall support.

Who is the audience? Instructional content, teaching style, and activities and practices must be suited to the interests and abilities of the participants:

- youth, including preschoolers, students, and drop-outs;

- educators;

- parents;

- community members, including seniors;

- staff, either paid or volunteer;

- other librarians.

What is the time frame? To meet the varying needs of users, and to address different contents adequately, instruction must accommodate different time frames:

- one-shot sessions such as talking about buying books for children;

- ongoing workshops on using equipment;

- in-service sessions on database management;

- series on storytelling or on vocational guidance;

- formal courses for library interns;

- brief instruction at the point of lending on genre reading.

What is the format? The library should provide a variety of learning modes to match the varying needs of user learning styles:

- speech or lecture;

- written documentation such as signs, packets, pamphlets, manuals, worksheets;

- audiovisual aids such as audiocassettes and videotapes;

- computer-based instruction.

What kind of recognitions should be given for participation?

- cards and certificates;

- permits and licenses (especially for computer use);

- premiums or incentives such as pencils or diskettes;

- grades.

Libraries can even contract with local universities to offer continuing-education units.

Instruction emphasizes the library's commitment to lifelong learning. High-quality instruction affirms the professional's expertise and the importance of libraries. And this translates into more financial support.

PROGRAMS

One way to hook users is to offer exciting and valuable programs. These events reinforce library resources and show how they can be applied in daily life—or can enrich living. Programming encourages links between the library and other groups, thus building support. Particularly in communities where culture is highly regarded, libraries can reflect cultural endeavors. Civilization does not come with a price tag, and budget-restricted libraries can offer exciting programs that answer people's needs for uplifting activity.

As with instruction, programs should serve a conscious purpose. Besides the educational objectives listed under "Instruction," programs can be used to accomplish mission goals.

Programs encourage use of library resources. Hold a business-people's "power breakfast" to point out library business resources. Conduct a children's story-hour workshop for local daycare providers. Invite local college counselors to a library program on college and career information in the library. These programs can foster interest-group involvement in the library. After a business workshop, one company donated needed furniture to the sponsoring library.

Programs increase public awareness. Offer a public forum to discuss local environmental issues. Hold a candidates' debate. Discuss library concerns in a town-meeting atmosphere. Particularly as libraries try to provide varied opinions about subjects, public-awareness programs will foster critical thinking.

Programs provide public service. Conduct family-literacy programs. Have doctors discuss teen-pregnancy issues. Let the local humane society offer free services for a day at the library. Because libraries constitute part of the community, they should support other community efforts.

Programs facilitate coalition building. Offer Black-History-Month programs, which are directed by church groups, A Better Chance (an educational program for African-American youth), and African-American cultural groups. Hold an environment fair to bring together youth organizations, conservation groups, nature lovers, and other related parties. By providing a focused theme, the library helps to coalesce groups that might not otherwise hold joint programs. These coalition groups can then support similar issues that affect the library. For instance, after a particular Black-history program occurred, the participants used the library more—and they developed a successful series of ongoing annual library programs.

As with instruction, programming comes in a variety of "flavors":

- poetry reading;

- color analysis;

- career exploration;

- youth summits on social issues;

- consciousness raising about rainforests;

- book collecting;

- fashion design;

- science magic;

- computer-generated animation;

- Chinese calligraphy.

Library programs demand thorough planning. Key elements include

- designing the content and delivery;

- setting up the program: getting the presenters and needed equipment;

- determining the time and the time frame;

- arranging for space (which may be away from the library);

- determining an entrance donation or fee;

- publicizing the program;

- obtaining supporting materials (food, paper, furniture);

- arranging for facility setup and cleanup;

- evaluating and following up on the program.

Especially with limited budgets, librarians should call upon other groups to plan and conduct these programs. The library contributes space and a captive audience; the sponsoring group supplies the content and publicity (in conjunction with the library). Prospective program groups include

- community interest groups (e.g., gardening groups, political organizations, etc.);

- speakers' bureaus (e.g., colleges, arts councils, chambers of commerce);

- educational groups (e.g., students, classes, clubs, faculty members, career counselors);

- service groups (e.g., 4-H, the American Red Cross, guide dogs, American Association of University Women, Rotary);

- traveling productions (e.g., museums, author tours, drama).

One caveat: When for-profit groups do programs in libraries, a sense of endorsement is implied. Because libraries should avoid such commercial ties, it is more ethical to invite a group of like businesses together to have a product fair. This way, the library is seen as providing a community consumer service: People have the chance to compare products equitably. Furthermore, because businesses welcome the opportunity to show off their goods, they are likely to pay for the chance. Voila! The library has an instant money-maker. Computer-related fairs, as an example, also reinforce the library's involvement in information technology. Other themes and groups include colleges, publishers, storytellers and other performers, and youth organizations.

THE ISSUE OF SERVICE LEVELS

Professional service is indicative of an effective library. When budgets are cut, the question arises, How will information service be affected?

One issue deals with the standard of service. Some circles advocate streamlined service for all; in that way more people can be helped. Others think that service should be as thorough as ever, even if it means fewer people will get assistance. The underlying concept of the former approach is increased productivity: How can librarians help users overcome specific frustrations so users can find materials themselves—and more users can be assisted? The latter argument points to the need of providing the best service possible so that users will maintain high expectations—and will demand additional professional staff.

Another issue relates to the level of librarianship training required to help users. Some librarians believe in a solid line dividing professional and paraprofessional functions. Others feel that service should be carried out by the person who has the minimum level of competence required. Those in the first group want to make sure that the highest standards of librarianship are maintained. They may also be afraid that if nonprofessionals, especially volunteers, can perform duties satisfactorily, then professionals may be replaced by less well-trained people. The latter group welcomes paraprofessional help because professionals can then deal with the more complex jobs. If well-trained volunteers can perform professional jobs, then more users can be helped.

A third issue focuses on cutting library hours effectively. One group advocates maximizing service by keeping the library open during high-demand periods. Others believe that prime hours should be cut to make people aware of their need for the library.

No single right answer exists for any of these critical issues. However, each action is based on a philosophical stance about service, and each action has specific consequences. The main point is that librarians need to use their mission statements to guide their philosophy of service. They need to decide which principles get the highest priorities: short-term or long-term goals, intensive or extensive performance. Whatever decisions they make, they need to justify them—and live with the results.

7

Public Relations

"Front Page" press hat

open mouth for constant sound bites

go-to-the-people sandwich board publicity

FREE BOOKS!

clapper for professional-looking multi-media productions

megaphone to maximize audio communication

stylish shoes for classy image

A near-zero library budget implies a poverty-stricken library. Money is an objective issue, but working in a poor library is an emotional situation. Crying poverty does not help people who are down on their luck, and self-pity does not help the impoverished library. Positive thinking does.

Especially in times of challenge, librarians should study the image that their libraries convey to the public and then work diligently to project a strong, positive image that people can identify with and support. How librarians communicate their situation helps determine whether that situation will improve or stagnate. A strong, proactive public-relations campaign can attract positive attention to — and increased financial backing for — the library.

A good working definition of *public relations* is given by the British Institute of Public Relations: "the deliberate, planned and sustained effort to establish and maintain mutual understanding between an organization and its publics." Key words include *planned, maintain, mutual understanding*, and *publics*. Public relations, PR, is not a one-time, shot in the dark. It is not one-directional. It is not a selling job. It is not targeted to one population. Rather, PR involves effective two-way communication between the library and all constituents.

In a way, all activities associated with the library can be potential public-relations vehicles. The PR component within libraries is the part that educates the constituents about the benefits of its services and responds to those constituents' needs and perceptions. Thus, public relations incorporates data gathering, planning, communication, and evaluation in an overall commitment to carry out the library's mission.

Public relations entails communicating regularly within the community in order to

- introduce and promote library services and resources;

- keep current on community services and resources;

- voice library and community needs;

- respond to needs;

- cooperate with the community in joint ventures;

- provide mutual support.

The best public relations, however, is still competent and friendly service. Enthusiastic librarians who genuinely love what they do and those they serve lay the groundwork for long-term library support.

WHAT IS COMMUNICATION?

In order to plan effective public-relations campaigns, librarians need to know what constitutes effective communication. Basically, the goal of communication is to share an idea or message, usually with the intention of motivating someone to action. But that goal is not accomplished easily.

The librarian must have a clear idea in mind. That idea is transformed into a message that is communicated through some medium or channel, be it words or images, and further refined to fit the target user's characteristics. The communications channel exists within a context of time, space, money, environment, and culture, any of which can distort the message. If the target users receive the message, it is hoped that they will respond and act upon it.

This abstract model can be exemplified concretely. Here is a simple PR effort with its components and possible results:

- Messenger: librarian;

- Idea or message: to explain the benefits of ILL;

- Ultimate goal: to increase ILL requests;

- Target audience: high-school students;

- Medium: spoken English;

- Context: 30-minute class visit to the library;

- Channel distortions: noise within the library, distracting displays, stuffy air or overworked air-conditioning, no seating, first sports rally following the visit;

- Audience distortions: language problem, hearing problem, mind focused on other issues, hunger, no pen or paper, restlessness;

- Possible reactions: none, positive ("Wow, I can find information for my report after all!"), negative ("This librarian is really boring."), neutral ("Yes, so?");

- Possible actions: none, request for ILL, question for clarification.

It is sometimes a wonder that anything gets accomplished! When planning a public-relations campaign, librarians need to determine the most effective communications channels to get across the specific idea to a specific targeted audience, and to minimize possible distortions.

EFFECTIVE COMMUNICATIONS

People are constantly bombarded by communication. What makes one message compelling and another ignored? Basically, the message must match the medium — and the audience. No single communications tool is ideal. Rather, each one has its advantages and disadvantages, which librarians need to recognize in order to maximize the impact of PR efforts.

A good exercise for a neophyte PR librarian is to study and evaluate an existing communications effort such as a magazine advertisement by asking these critical questions:

- What is my immediate response to this ad? Why?

- What elements about the communications triggered my response? Why?

- Does this message appeal to my emotions or to my intellect?

- Why was this medium chosen for the message?

- Is the medium the best vehicle to deliver the idea effectively? Why?

- In what context would this ad message work — or not work? Why?

- Which audience would respond to it most effectively? Why?

- What are its strengths and weaknesses?

- How could it be applied or modified to work in my library?

In general, studying advertising messages is a useful way to learn how professionals use words and images to capture attention, communicate value, and stimulate desire, all of which are important to get users to support the library.

A WORD ABOUT WORDS

Words are the mainstay of communication. Different formats require modification of the same concepts; here are some underlying principles that drive effective written and oral communication:

- Use clear, concise words.

- Follow formal grammar and spelling rules.

- Convey sincerity and conviction.

- Get the audience's attention immediately.

- Create and sustain interest.

- Create images through words.

- Organize words and ideas in logical sequence.

- Be credible and complete.

- Close with a call to action.

- Fit the message to the audience.

WRITTEN DOCUMENTS

One obvious advantage of written documentation is graphics. Unlike audio communication, written forms can take advantage of visual arrangement to further library messages. In addition, written communication is a permanent record that can be examined repeatedly in the future. If the message is strong and viable, written public relations can make a positive lasting impression. Here are some inexpensive ways to make a good impression in writing.

Present reports to state the library's cause in depth. The report can communicate an image, highlight a unique service or need, and sell the library to readers.

Create brochures to build awareness about the library, to complement presentations, to leave as a permanent reinforcer to hand out, and to use as mailers. Brochures should have lively copy, communicative graphics, and a clean look.

Develop instructional guides to complement personal advice; distribute these widely to related information agencies to reinforce library aid.

Write newsletters to inform interest groups, such as Friends of the Library, of progress and upcoming events. Two approaches succeed: Widespread distribution builds membership and a sense of inclusion. Limited distribution implies a sense of exclusiveness so that newsletter recipients feel they have an inside track on information.

Press releases send the library's message to the community. News items reflect time-sensitive, novel happenings. PR releases provide a novel spin on new or intriguing library services or needs. A photo can be included with the press release or sent separately as a photo release with an informative caption attached. Photo opportunities increase library visibility both literally and figuratively.

Some ways to cut down on printing costs include

- using postcards instead of letters to reduce postage;

- giving duplicating companies camera-ready copy;

- getting others to pay for duplication or soliciting paid advertising;

- taking advantage of batch runs to get low-cost color printing;

- using lighter-weight paper or end runs of colored paper;

- using volunteers instead of printers to collate or fold paper.

An accurate, regularly maintained mailing list is one of the library's most valuable assets for both press releases and newsletter mailings. Selective mailings describing a specific need or financial emergency can generate donations.

AUDIO

How do people communicate daily? By talking. Speech becomes a public-relations communication tool when it is used consciously to increase mutual understanding. Normal conversation affects how the public views librarians. Formal audio "products" offer a way to reach a wider audience with a sense of immediacy and drama. The key to successful verbal communication is conveying messages articulately and confidently. Good speaking stimulates good listening. For example, when librarians can incorporate prior discussions into their presentations, their audiences are truly captured. Another advantage of speech is that it costs nothing. Here are some good public-relations scenarios.

Give speeches to community groups, board meetings, and at other libraries. A speech is actually a two-way process. Both the speaker and the audience give of themselves: The speaker gives time and effort in preparation and delivery and the audience gives time and attention. Groups will often follow up an effective speech with a donation.

Give interviews on radio or public-access television shows. Note that interviews can be confrontational, so librarians should prepare thoroughly, remain friendly and objective, and keep a specific message in mind to convey as the interview progresses.

Make telephone calls for immediate feedback. The one disadvantage is that telephones are overused and their use may be discredited.

Use public-service announcements as a free means to communicate library concerns and opportunities.

Produce audiocassette recordings to use on radio shows. Most stations have programs for not-for-profit organizations.

VISUALS

Pictures are the first stimuli that people respond to. A key graphic image commands instant attention—but it can also be instantly dismissed unless reinforced with meaningful content. Visual-heavy media such as posters should carry a simple message that is conveyed arrestingly and esthetically and that has emotional impact.

Pictures are a staple PR item because they stimulate the viewer and communicate quickly. Moreover, illustrating concepts through art, photography, charts and graphs, and cartoons helps break down library barriers for the non-English reader or illiterate persons. Keep a good stock of pictures on hand for displays, instruction, clip art, collages, greeting cards, even instant wrapping paper. To keep them in good order, classify them and mount them. Free sources of pictures abound:

- old magazines and calendars;

- used postcards and greeting cards;

- student and adult artwork;

- library mail, which is filled with promotional pictures and illustrated catalogs.

Posters combine a single message and an attention-getting graphic element on a large scale. Some posters serve as quick reminders, and others serve as one-stop learning stations with lots of text and concepts. Posters can be placed throughout the community and are visible 24 hours a day, so they constitute a good outreach public-relations strategy. Some uses of posters include

- announcements for upcoming programs;

- high-profile booklists;

- graphic representations of statistics;

- easy-to-read directions for library activities;

- a focus point for reading programs;

- alternative bulletin boards.

Posters can be made from cardboard boxes, wrapping paper, even cloth. Posting student-made posters shows the library's involvement with the community—and encourages community support.

Signs are underrated as communications tools. Signs provide a major key to library access. Their importance should be affirmed by having high-quality signage. All signs should be highly visible and highly legible. All signs having a similar purpose, such as directional or instructional, should look similar: the same color, type face, and dimension. Signs need not be expensive to look good; simple computer programs such as Print Shop quickly produce attractive signs that when printed on colored paper make for a readable and professional-looking signage system. Some creative ways to work with signs include

- painting oversized signs on doors or walls;

- using banners as signs;

- sticking vinyl lettering on shelving;

- using a unifying theme or graphic to tie signs together conceptually;

- creating minisigns for tables and other small display areas.

MULTIMEDIA

Multimedia combine two or more media to produce an exciting communications message. Theoretically, the complexity of producing a high-quality multimedia production is offset by its dramatic impact — and by the ability to use it to reach many populations.

Displays constitute the basic multimedia communication tool because they combine visuals and text, can incorporate movement or simulations, and can be placed in high-visibility locations. Ideally, viewers see the main idea immediately and interact with display elements to absorb more detailed concepts. Displays serve

- as learning stations for group or individual work;

- as motivators to encourage reading or pursuing an interest;

- as ways to share information visually;

- as ways to combine several media in a unified manner; and

- as means to make the library attractive and dynamic.

Basic esthetic factors should guide display creation. To make displays exciting as well as attractive, use the mobile approach with three-dimensional objects and moving parts. Place displays in distinctive settings: on poles, on empty chairs, on shelves, hanging from the ceiling. Dynamic displays can be as inexpensive as other visual formats.

- Group cardboard boxes together and cover them with a lively cloth, then arrange the display on top.

- Fill an up-side-down umbrella with rainy-day reading.

- On a counter surround stand-up art books or Japanese materials with origami figures.

- Attach display materials to flexible cardboard.

- Build a display around a game board or map.

- Draw an enlarged comic strip display to illustrate a concept.

- Search bookstores and other businesses for thrown-out display cases and stands.

Probably the next cheapest multimedia format is videotape. Librarians can use public-access-channel video crews to produce a lively production that dramatizes library needs. Many libraries tape their own shows using community volunteer help. Such local support affirms library efforts. In one case, a young-adults librarian sponsored a teen video crew, who documented the library's successful Sci Fi convention and garnered extra community visibility and support as a result. A classic multimedia presentation is the slide-tape show, which has two distinct advantages: It is portable, and it can be changed or modified fairly easily to fit a specific audience.

Other combination media include computer-based products such as HyperCard, CD-ROM, laserdiscs; and live productions, which are featured in chapter 8. As communications tools become more advanced technologically, the options for multimedia public relations will increase.

THE PLANNING PROCESS

For a PR campaign to succeed, librarians should first determine what action or outcome is desired and, second, decide what message is the most important one to give. Planning should include user input gleaned from evaluating the present situation and assessing what is needed. Only then can librarians determine what communication tools to use.

This approach includes a postevaluation of how well communication was accomplished and modifications to the process to improve future communication. Librarians should evaluate the content for its usefulness and its accuracy. They should examine the message's format or medium in terms of its style, connotations, and ability to engage the audience. They should also observe the channel's context to identify factors that lessen the message's impact or distort it. As the final test, librarians should study the audience's response in terms of the degree of emotional and intellectual involvement. Ultimately, all public-relations efforts should be evaluated in terms of cost-effective results: Was the outlay of time and resources worth the return?

Although one-shot publicity may be better than none, a carefully thought-out campaign or theme promotion over a period of time is more effective because it combines individual efforts to different targeted populations into a unified package of consistent calls to action. All pieces in the campaign should have the same theme and the same look: consistent logo, typeface, color combination, graphics.

LET SOMEONE ELSE DO
THE SPADEWORK

Having a limited budget usually means having limited time. How can librarians take the time to plan and implement extensive PR campaigns? The answer: Use other people's expertise. Public relations follows standard procedures, so librarians can model their efforts on existing success stories. Although copyright laws and ethical considerations should guide such "borrowing," librarians can adapt programs and individual PR pieces to fit their own situations without much trouble.

Read the literature. The American Library Association annually publishes the John Cotton Dana award-winning PR campaigns, which exemplify high-quality results. Professional journals recount successful PR efforts. For general approaches, read books by public-relations professionals.

Examine professional PR products. Library associations and suppliers publish catalogs of their PR materials. Take hints from the professionals and design original works that tell a specific message for a specific library. Keep an open mind—and an open eye. Public-relations ideas abound. One librarian used a mystery motif found in such a publication. She tailored it for a week-long library celebration. Using the theme "Take the mystery out of the library," the librarian adapted Clue game concepts to present a daily murder mystery. She gave library clues about the murderer, victim, place, and weapon for her students to solve. For example,

- Victim: Bay of Pigs instigator

- Murderer: Russian sympathizer

- Place: home of the cowboys

- Weapon: fusil

She also daily copied one-page mysteries from *Murder, Inc.* for students to solve. All contest participants received mystery bookmarks and had a chance to enter a library raffle. Winners received food prizes (food being a major motivator). To complement the contests, the librarian displayed mystery books. Needless to say, the campaign was successful.

Representative thematic images include

- animals;

- the environment: rainforests, recycling;

- fictional characters and genres;

- technology;

- ethnic and cultural groups;

- periods in history;

- travel and foreign lands;

- recreation.

Use professional PR consultants. With enough networking, librarians can sometimes induce public-relations experts to donate their time to assist campaign efforts. Technical assistance time is costly, so for these professionals to be effective, librarians need to be open to expert suggestions and be prepared ahead of time with specifics about

- public-relations goals;

- target audiences;

- time frame;

- feasible communications pieces;

- budget (zero?).

A PUBLIC-RELATIONS MIND-SET
IN A SCHOOL

Suppose a school librarian wants to promote information skills through computer technology. Here are some ways to use a PR mind-set to accomplish this goal:

- Inventory all the software and equipment within the school and integrate the list into the library's catalog. Serve as a guide for others to locate these resources.

- Provide evaluation criteria for faculty in selecting appropriate computer technology.

- Suggest computer software acquisitions for other departments.

- Maintain a strong collection of computer-related catalogs and promote them.

- Subscribe to computer-related books and journals. Promote them and make them accessible to others. Note articles of interest particular to faculty members or administrators and invite them to read the material in the library.

- Conduct in-service workshops or orientations about computer-related subjects for students, faculty, parents, community members.

- Demonstrate effective software programs—and effective ways to use them.

- Produce computer-generated publications for the library and the school.

- Troubleshoot computer use for the school community.

- Train others in database search strategies. Conduct searches for faculty and administrators.

- Use telecommunications systems to expand and improve interlibrary searching and loaning.

- Participate in educational bulletin boards and promote them.

Even with limited knowledge about computer technology, librarians can develop effective public-relations strategies to improve information use.

CHAPTER

8

Fund-Raising

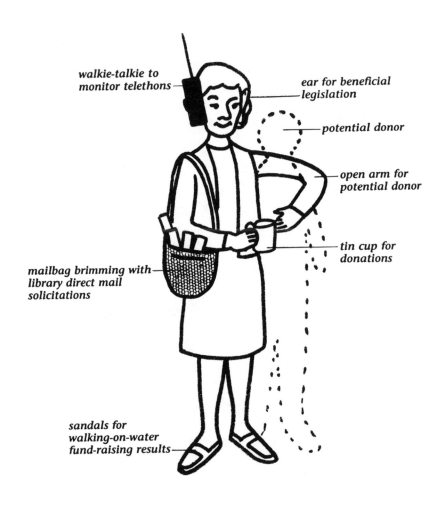

walkie-talkie to
monitor telethons

ear for beneficial
legislation

potential donor

open arm for
potential donor

tin cup for
donations

mailbag brimming with
library direct mail
solicitations

sandals for
walking-on-water
fund-raising results

Libraries should be adequately and permanently funded by their governing bodies, right? They should not be run on "soft" funding. But in the real world of the 1990s this is not necessarily the case. Even with adequate funding, and certainly for underbudgeted libraries, occasional fund-raising can help in specially targeted areas or to meet temporary needs. The effort that librarians make today in raising enrichment money to further their missions demonstrates an extra degree of professional commitment that demands an equal demonstration of support from governing bodies.

PURPOSEFUL FUND-RAISING

Before librarians raise money, they should have a specific purpose for doing so. A concrete benefit should guide each fund-raising effort. Some typical purposes, which fit into mission statements, include

- filling subject gaps, such as science or foreign languages;

- increasing human resources, such as project aides;

- implementing special projects, such as retrospective conversion cataloging;

- getting seed money to start a special collection or service.

As librarians determine a purpose for fund-raising, they need to ask themselves several questions:

- How will users benefit?

- How long will benefits last?

- How will the library be improved?

- How much will it cost?

- Is the library prepared for fund-raising with upfront money, sufficient time and resources, a positive attitude, and commitment?

- How will funds be raised? Why?

Focused fund-raising efforts help librarians accomplish one goal well; scattered goals can water down the effort and weaken the impact. Therefore, librarians should prioritize their efforts either according to need or to the probability of fund-raising success. However, placing all one's hopes on one effort is dangerous. The ideal approach is focused diversification: one or two focused goals supported by several targeted fund-raising efforts. Some things work, some things do not, but keep at it.

GETTING HELP

Librarians cannot raise money alone, nor should they. By involving other people in fund-raising, librarians garner support and facilitate user "ownership" in the fund-raiser and in the end goal of the fund-raising effort. Other people can plan and carry out fundraisers, and they can recruit still others to help. Of course, the governing body should know about any fund-raising efforts and solidly support library actions.

Potential fund-raising assistants include

- library staff;

- other personnel within the institution or organization;

- board members;

- users;

- Friends of the Library;

- development offices;

- school or community clubs and special-interest groups;

- service organizations.

It is one task to identify helpers. It is another to enlist and motivate them. Interestingly, library fund-raising helpers often become the biggest donors. That is because they believe in the library and the benefit that the fund-raiser makes possible. So the best way to motivate people to help is to get them excited about the purpose of the fund-raiser.

Next, these fund-raiser assistants need to work on campaign specifics. The more the fund-raiser is planned, the easier it is to match jobs with helper capabilities and interests. In fact, unless the librarian has a crackerjack fund-raiser on board already, planning should precede any recruitment, because each volunteer needs a concrete job to get started on right away.

As with other volunteers, fund-raising assistants need appropriate supervision, generous praise, timely correction, and proper recognition. Reward them with a certificate or mention their names in brochures or news releases. Once a first-time fund-raiser succeeds, he can help evaluate efforts and document his steps for future fund-raisers. If the fund-raiser was worthwhile — and fun — volunteers are likely to come back for more!

SOURCES OF FUNDING

Time for facts: The biggest donors are individuals rather than foundations or businesses. However, every potential source should be appealed to. With this caveat, here are some possible funding sources.

Many of the same people who help with fund-raisers are good source of funds themselves: board members, users, Friends of the Library, development offices, clubs and special-interest groups, service organizations. It should be noted that the first donors are usually the biggest, for they start the campaign rolling and motivate others to equal their financial contributions.

Those people influenced by the school give because they know the school and have benefited from it: graduates, families, friends.

Sometimes these donors' employers offer matching funds for non-profit (as in library!) contributions. This approach has the added benefit of stimulating donors to act.

Community members contribute to better the library, thereby improving their own community: homeowners, businesses, local service and social organizations.

Public and school libraries are eligible for government funding and may not be aware of special funds available for specific users or purposes. (It should be noted that independent schools can usually get federal funds, but they may be excluded from receiving state or local funds. These librarians need to research eligibility requirements carefully.) Some government sources and documents to research include

- U.S. Department of Education Chapter 1 funds for disadvantaged student populations, general Chapter 2 funds, and many specialized funds for school improvement, bilingual programs and others;

- Library Services and Construction Act, with several subprovisions;

- National Science Foundation for math and science projects;

- State Arts and Humanities councils, which usually choose priority projects each year;

- Short-term state funds for designated programs, such as California's Tobacco Fund for materials to encourage nonsmoking;

- Local Education Funds centers, found in large urban areas with significant low-income and minority populations.

Professional associations offer grants and awards for research, public relations, model programs, and special projects. Often these associations get cosponsorship from businesses.

Private foundations and companies offer grants and awards for special projects. Typically, each foundation has a favorite topic and a geographic preference, and they often ask for matching funds to prove local support. One example is World Book, which contributes one dollar toward encyclopedia purchases for every two dollars raised locally. One the local level, businesses sometimes "adopt" a school or library.

Librarians should keep files of possible donors (or have their fund-raising volunteers maintain these files). Information may be kept on fill-in form sheets, index cards, or computer database for easy storage and retrieval. Some kinds of useful information to garner include

- general information: name, address, age, sex, employment, family, memberships, hobbies and interests, other charities;

- library-specific information: donation history, library interests, library services used, types of books or other resources used;

- donation records: contact person, kind of contribution, dates, follow-ups, recognitions, referral names.

HOW TO ASK

The most effective way to ask for money is to first establish a working relationship with the potential donor. By developing a sense of interest and trust, donors feel that they are partners with librarians, each helping the other. Then asking for donations becomes part of the total reciprocity process.

One secret for getting money is to ask for it from the right person at the right time for the right reason. People give for a variety of reasons:

- fear of losing good reading material or cultural activities;

- investment for their children's education or the community's future;

- gratitude for remembered or current benefits gained from library use or from librarian help;

- pride in being a part of the library's success or in personal achievement.

The actual request, whether in person or in writing, should include these points:

- Ask for a specific amount (aim high).

- Give a specific purpose for the money.

- Explain the time-sensitive need to convey a sense of urgency.

- Demonstrate the library's track record.

- Tell how the donor will benefit personally.

- Help the donor visualize the results of the donation (e.g., special collection being used by local groups).

- Answer possible donor obstacles with solutions.

- Give the donor options (e.g., type of recognition, record of donation).

If you are soliciting a contribution in person, obtaining a donation, or at least a commitment to donate, at that time is optimal because the potential donor still has your goals and needs in mind. If you are calling on potential donors in their homes, know when to leave. Be sure to thank the donor in writing with a certificate or membership card. Put the donor on a donor mailing list, because once contributors trust the librarian and see the concrete benefits of giving, they will donate again and again.

When personal contact is not possible or feasible, another option is to write an effective request letter. The letter should attract attention, appeal to the emotions and the mind, cover the previous request points, and thank the donor in advance. Naturally, writing should be clear, sincere, and attractive. Pictures help the reader visualize the goal.

Direct-mail advertisers have fine-tuned this approach. They know that targeted letters are cost-effective, particularly because efforts can be evaluated by the responses received—and by those not returned. A successful direct-mail campaign also lays the foundation for future fund-raising plans by providing names for a donors list.

Six elements make up a complete letter kit.

1. An enticing outside envelope with first-class postage should be used because it makes the request stand out from the junk mail. If the fund-raiser is for a school library, let the student carry the request home; this saves postage and involves the main beneficiary of an improved library.

2. A solicitation letter details the fund-raiser: the library, the project, the benefit, and the cost. A one-page letter is easy for the recipient to read; a good two- or four-page letter has room to tell the reader the full story. If possible, the letter should be hand-signed by the librarian. A hand-written postscript in a different-colored pen offers an additional personal touch and repeats the fund-raiser goal.

3. An additional short note provides that extra appeal that can tip the donation scale in favor of the library. It should highlight the benefit resulting from the contribution and should be signed by a board member or other important participant.

4. An additional useful enclosure, with pictures, if possible, is a short brochure describing the library.

5. A pledge card with self-addressed return envelope constitutes the library's call to action and permits the respondant to choose the type and level of contribution. For example, contributors can donate a subscription, a book, a computer program, or a check. List a series of dollar amounts on the pledge card, with check boxes. The lowest amount noted establishes the library's expectation level, so dollar amounts should reflect the dimension of the fund-raiser. Even if respondants send no contribution at that point, their names and addresses should become part of the library's mailing list for future reference.

6. Offer a premium to the respondant. People like to receive concrete evidence of their action. An attractive little publication, set of cards, bookmark, or certificate reinforces the literacy role.

LIBRARY FUND-RAISING PROJECTS

Libraries can develop a wide variety of fund-raising efforts. With a purpose in mind and potential donors listed, librarians can choose how they want to raise money and enlist others to help. As with any other plan, details should include

- resources: space, human, material;

- time frame: one-shot, annual, periodic, ongoing;

- publicity;

- donor fulfillment: receipts, thank-yous, follow-up;

- evaluation.

One successful approach is the annual fund-raiser. A yearly solicitation requires a well-developed relationship between libraries and their communities: "friend-raising" precedes fund-raising. Libraries need to be presented as friends: the librarian as a special person and users as neighbors. Library service should be illustrated by personal anecdotes. Generating annual giving requires a committed planning group that can take care of mailings and telephone solicitations. Although an annual fund-raiser can be time-consuming, it can build a base of support that can be counted upon in following years. Libraries can also become part of a larger organizational annual campaign; in that situation donors can designate the library as the gift recipient.

Libraries can sell products. Libraries can theoretically sell candy or cakes, but the following products reinforce the library's professional image:

- postal and note cards of the library, of collection excerpts (with copyright permission);

- computer-customized greeting cards;

- bound blank books;

- calligraphy: posters, cards, custom items;

- prints and posters;

- calendars;

- bookmarks;

- library-produced videotapes;

- library-produced publications (local history is particularly salable);

- library-logo bookbags and T-shirts (required cash investments may be covered by business donations).

Libraries can sell services. Naturally, librarians should not make users pay for services that are normally provided gratis. The governing body must approve the service and be sure that no conflict of interest occurs.

Typical services that library staff can perform include

- original video- and audiotaping and duplicating;

- off-site storytelling;

- book selection;

- training of interest groups;

- tutoring;

- research;

- renting facilities or equipment;

- computer-related services: graphics work, publications editing and production;

- organizing children's parties.

Libraries can hold events themselves or participate in larger, communitywide events. In the former case, libraries can gather interested exhibitors and charge them for booths. In the latter case, libraries themselves get a booth and sell their products. In either case events should attract local interest and entertain attendees. A theme helps the public to identify the event. In one fund-raiser, librarians had fun playing in an exhibition basketball game benefit with disabled students; the public relations engendered by the game helped both the teens and the librarians. Other successful event formats include

- exhibits of art, fashion, publications;

- film festivals;

- benefits;

- computer camps;

- shows with speakers or performers;

- fairs;

- carnivals;

- picnics;

- dining and dancing;

- student breakfast clubs or camp-ins;

- readathons (students get pledges for the number of pages read);

- senior-center and senior-citizens events;

- intergenerational activities;

- auctions.

Several libraries have considerable success with auctions where their users ask celebrities to donate personal items for auctioning: shoes, books, autographs, memorabilia. Also libraries can collect items and recover money for returning grocery coupons, paper, or used computers.

GETTING GRANTS

Applying for grants is hard work, and grants can be hard to get. So why bother? For experience and power and to improve the library—that's why. Obviously, the more times one applies, the better one gets at writing grants. Also, the more often a name appears, the better chance that name will collect the money.

As for power, receiving a grant opens doors. Receiving a grant implies competence, a good track record, legitimacy—which leads to getting other grants. Successful grantees receive positive publicity for the library and are also more apt to get additional awards.

So the question now becomes, How do I write a grant? Probably the first step is to identify possible donors. The more local the granting agency, the more likely it is that the librarian can approach it personally. Also, on a local level, less competition exists. Only after exhausting this level should librarians try for regional, state, or national grants.

Identifying grant sources is work in itself. Neighboring libraries may carry books on writing grants and on funding sources. The most inclusive list is maintained by Federal Foundation Centers. In fact, the group has 10 regional offices throughout the United States where anyone can get immersed in funding documentation.

Some listings are general, some are specific by discipline, approach, or candidate qualifications. Librarians need to read funding agencies' descriptions carefully.

- How often do they give?

- What are their main funding causes?

- What are grantee qualifications?

- How much money is available, in total and for a typical grant?

- Who has received grants in the past from them?

Libraries must meet all agency requirements before even thinking of applying. Sometimes it helps to send for grant guidelines.

Getting grant money is a matter of matching library needs with the grant focus. The closer the match, the better the chance of receiving money. So the librarian must look at the library's and users' needs relative to the potential funder's goals. Probably the most efficient way to approach getting grants is to begin with a generalized project and then tailor it to the desired granting source.

Of course, the integrity of the project must be maintained; if one applies for money just to get money, the effort often backfires. Either the library will not succeed or it will be stuck with a project that users do not need or want. It *does* make sense, though, to discover what areas are generally "hot," perhaps disabled persons, at-risk students, minority users, computer studies, or in-service training.

Before writing the proposal, the librarian should gather information about the library's background and legitimacy. Most funders want to see a history of operation. They want to make sure the library is not a fly-by-night applicant. Audit records are very useful documentation, as is a short descriptive brochure.

The next step is to write the grant proposal itself. All information must be included in the same sequence that it is requested in the guidelines. That usually entails a summary of project intent, budget, source of matching funds (showing financial backing from associated parties), letters of commendation, and financial statements.

The most creative part, of course, is the intent. Specificity counts. It helps to incorporate the production of some kind of tangible product. How is the project unique, and can it serve as a model for other locations and situations? How will the project benefit the funder? A tidy, well-constructed grant proposal will be looked on more favorably than will a pie-in-the-sky idea. And, naturally, all proposals should be neat and accurate in appearance.

Librarians must also document their own qualifications: experience, expertise, contacts, authority, influence. Librarians should focus on their unique strengths. Why is the librarian the logical choice to implement the project?

Most proposals should include an evaluation section. Does the project make a difference? How will progress be measured? Evaluations should be objective, specific, and measurable. Proposals are stronger if some sort of pilot testing or peer evaluation has been conducted already.

It can be useful to have others review the proposal: for example, a local congressperson for a federal grant. Sometimes someone in the know can tell if the proposal is on track. Some people suggest hand-carrying the proposal to the decisionmakers. Librarians need to know themselves well enough to know if their physical presence will further the library cause. Some librarians have a grant insider to introduce the proposal; that person should be well respected and authoritative. Usually, though, once the proposal is in the hands of the decision-makers, librarians should sit back and wait. Steady inquiries only hurt the cause.

Where are some places to start looking for grant information?

- public libraries;

- successful grantees;

- foundation centers;

- conferences (and networks);

- publications and announcements;

- professional organizations;

- university bulletin boards.

Finally, the librarian might want to consider joint fund-raising efforts with other departments. One high school library has a history of successful cooperation. A couple of factors facilitated the relationship: 1) the mathematics department directs the instructional computer laboratory; 2) the librarian had taught computer programming and was credentialed in mathematics. In brief, common interests and competencies made the librarian more credible to department members. Library fund-raising efforts went hand-in-hand with other departmental efforts. Of three grants applied for, all three were received.

The first project was a grant written by the librarian, new to the job, to acquire computer technology for the library. With careful purchasing, the math department was able to gain two Apple IIe computers from the grant. A second successful grant, initiated by the math department, focused on geometry manipulatives. The librarian helped write the grant and included a request for supporting books for the library. A third grant request took advantage of a nearby school that was closing. The math department acquired its Macintosh lab, and the library received four machines. The computer teacher installed utility programs in the library equipment and troubleshoots as needed.

LOBBYING

For critical financial situations in a town or in a large county system, librarians may need to enlist government help through special bonds. Such measures require extensive planning and outside consultant expertise. Libraries need to have a long-standing, healthy reputation within the community and broad-based support. Furthermore, librarians need to know the legislative process — and the legislators.

Before embarking on seeking initiatives from government, librarians should practice lobbying for their causes. They can provide valuable service to legislators and other elected officials by providing facts and figures and voicing community concerns. Librarians can write to or talk with decisionmakers or join other lobbying groups. Lobbying, like fund-raising, is a long-term commitment.

9

When Your Budget Is Increased

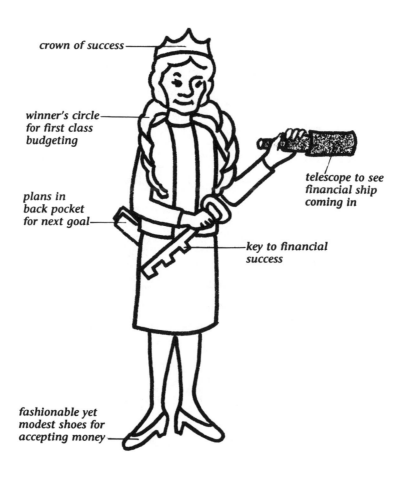

crown of success

winner's circle for first class budgeting

plans in back pocket for next goal

telescope to see financial ship coming in

key to financial success

fashionable yet modest shoes for accepting money

When the sails of the Good Ship Budget come into view, librarians must exert as much effort as when no ship was in sight on the horizon. When library budget increases are the result of long-term, hard-won effort, everyone expects to see a visible improvement in the library. If service and resources do not change, money will not keep coming.

Therefore, librarians should always stand prepared with a wish list of resources. When funds are allocated, librarians should get those purchase orders out the door immediately—and follow up on any delayed deliveries. When items arrive, librarians should process them quickly and then highly publicize their availability, linking the new acquisitions to the increased funding.

Librarians must also plan for any accommodations needed for the materials added when funding arrives. Is the site prepared for computer installation? Is shelving adequate for a special collection? If magazine subscriptions double, can display space hold the added issues? Although it may seem frustrating to take the time to plan for new resources that may never come, it is even more embarrassing to be unprepared when they *do* arrive!

Increased budgets also require adjustments in budget planning. Priorities may need changing; for instance, if a new CD-ROM drive is donated, the budget should provide money for CD-ROM products. If an extensive career or college collection is acquired, library service may change as "futures" workshops and employment services are added.

Changes in budget may also entail changes in librarian attitudes. "Think poor" librarians may react by going on a spending spree—or by continuing to be as penurious as ever, not rising to the positive changes in funding. Increased in budgets are cause for celebration—but then, back to more serious immediate business. As much as possible, librarians should make short-term and long-term projections so that they can plan revenues and expenditures realistically. Be prepared.

Follow-up is a cornerstone of continuing financial support. Librarians need to

- thank donors and decisionmakers;

- reexamine the library's mission statement and objectives;

- reevaluate library standards of service and resources;

- broaden the library's support base;

- plan the next fund-raising project.

Finally, no matter what the budget level, librarians should remain competent and enthusiastic. As they maintain effective public relations with their constituents, keeping current on needs and resources, librarians lay the groundwork for future budget expansion, which can make their vision of the best library a reality.

Bibliography

American Association of School Librarians and the Association for Educational Communication and Technology. *Information Power: Guidelines for School Library Media Programs.* Chicago: American Library Association, 1988.

The new standard for maximizing library program effectiveness.

Anderson, Pauline. *Planning School Library Media Facilities.* Hamden, CT: Shoe String, 1990.

Field-tested ways to make the most of library space.

Belcher, Jane C., and Julia M. Jacobsen. *From Idea to Funded Project: Grant Proposals that Work.* 4th ed. Phoenix, AZ: Oryx, 1992.

Steps for successful funding, from developing the project to evaluating its impact.

Boss, Richard W. *Grant Money and How to Get It: a Handbook for Librarians.* New York: Bowker, 1980.

A classic title on grantsmanship.

Breivik, Patricia Senn, and E. Burr Gibson. *Funding Alternatives for Libraries.* Chicago: American Library Association, 1979.

How to overcome financial obstacles.

Christensen, Ann, and Lee Green. *Trash to Treasures.* Littleton, CO: Libraries Unlimited, 1982.

Practical tips for recycling the old into attractive "new."

Costa, Betty, and Marie Costa. *A Micro Handbook for Small Libraries and Media Centers.* 3d ed. Englewood, CO: Libraries Unlimited, 1991.

The standard text for beginning technology librarians.

Daly, Nancy R. "Planning for Action." *Association Management* (August 1991): 128-131.

Good points for making financial points with key decision-makers.

Fox, Beth Wheeler. *Dynamic Community Libraries: Creative, Practical and Inexpensive Ideas for the Director.* Chicago: American Library Association, 1988.

Tips on resource reserves, fund-raising, public relations, and planning.

Gardner, Marilyn. "Readers Become Noisy Advocates." *Christian Science Monitor* (9 July 1991): 14.

A community success story: how the public saved their library.

Hayes, Sherman, and Donald Brown. "Creative Budgeting and Funding for Automation: Getting the Goods!" *Wilson Library Bulletin* (April 1992): 42-43.

Concentrated article on ways to acquire computer resources for the library.

Kawasaki, Guy. "The Ten Best Ways to Get a Macintosh into Your Company." *Apple Library Users Group Newsletter* (October 1991): 97-98.

Targeted, practical tips that can be applied to library settings.

LaRue, James. "Shopping Around." *Wilson Library Bulletin* (April 1992): 88-89.

How to do effective comparison shopping.

Laughlin, Mildred Knight, and Kathy Howard Latrobe. *Public Relations for School Library Media Centers.* Englewood, CO: Libraries Unlimited, 1990.

Practitioners in the field offer ideas to implement communications plans.

Levinson, Jay Conrad. *Guerilla Marketing.* Boston: Houghton Mifflin, 1984.

A no-holds barred approach to identifying key markets and profiting from them.

Pichette, William. "Protecting the Budget—and Your Position, Too!" *Book Report* (January 1983): 20-23.

Using finances to improve the library and staffing situation.

PR Notebook for School Librarians. Worthington, OH: Linworth, 1991.

Book Report articles on planning, targeted constituents, various communications channels, and activities.

Prentice, Ann E. *Financial Planning for Libraries.* Metuchen, NJ: Scarecrow, 1983.

An in-depth approach to various budgeting issues.

Reed, Mary Hutchings. *Copyright Primer for Librarians and Educators.* Chicago: American Library Association, 1987.

Useful guide on copying, especially in litigious times.

Roberts, Anne F., and Susan Griswold Blandy. *Public Relations for Librarians.* Englewood, CO: Libraries Unlimited, 1989.

A basic guide to increase and improve the library image.

Small, Adeline Mercer, and Diana Rovena Jones. *Free Magazines for Libraries.* 3d ed. Jefferson, NC: McFarland, 1989.

Guide to valuable resources, with core lists.

Smallwood, Carol. *Free Resource Building for Librarians and Teachers.* 2d ed. Jefferson, NC: McFarland, 1992.

Subject bibliography of inexpensive sources for classroom and school libraries.

Smith, G. Stevenson. *Managerial Accounting for Libraries and Other Not-for-Profit Organizations.* Chicago: American Library Association, 1991.

Cost control and project evaluation methods to help decision makers.

Spencer, Michael. *Free Publications from U.S. Government Agencies.* Englewood, CO: Libraries Unlimited, 1989.

Descriptions of government agencies and their publications.

Steele, Victoria, and Stephen D. Elder. *Becoming a Funraiser.* Chicago: American Library Association, 1992.

Thorough principles and practices in library development.

Tecker, Glenn H. *Symposium for Chief Elected Officers and Chief Staff Executives.* Washington, D.C.: American Society of Association Executives, 1992.

A set of practical readings to accompany a workshop for non-profit organizations.

White, Virginia. *Grant Proposals that Succeeded.* New York: Plenum, 1983.

Success stories and ways to replicate them.

INDEX

displays, 9, 19, 21-23, 25, 40-41, 67, 71, 90-92
distributors, 37-39, 43, 45, 50, 52-53
dividers, 16-17, 19, 23
donations, 28, 33-34, 64, 68, 78, 102-6, 108
Duplicates Exchange Union, 40

Econo-Clad Books, 37
Education, U.S. Department of, 102
Educational Material Clearinghouse, 39
educators. *See* teachers
Educators Progress Series, 39
Edward R. Hamilton, 37
electronic bulletin boards, 44, 55, 65, 96
electronic mail, 55-56
environment, 77-78
ethics, 39, 43-45, 95
evaluation, 5-9, 13, 79, 95, 110, 116
events. *See* programs
external forces, 7

Federal Foundation Centers, 109
fields (databases), 56-58
file cabinets, 27
Financial Planning for Libraries, 13
flooring, 20
foundations, 102, 109, 111
FredWriter, 55
Free Materials for Schools and Libraries, 39
freeware, 55

Friends of the Library, 28-29, 38, 61, 64-66, 68, 87, 100-101, 106. *See also* interest groups
fund-raising, 64-65, 66, 99-111
furniture, 16-17, 19, 26, 28-29, 48

Gardner, Marilyn, 68
Gateway 2000, 52
General Services Administration, 29
Girl Scouts, 4
government, 29, 37, 102, 109, 112. *See also* specific agencies
Government Printing Office, 37
grants, 109-11
groups. *See* interest groups, organizations, users groups

hardware, 51-52
Hotho & Co., 37
HyperCard, 72, 92

IBM, 51, 57
Information Power, 3, 13
Ingram, 36
instruction, 51, 74-76, 84-85, 87, 90
interest groups, 64-66, 77, 100-101. *See also* Friends of the Library
interlibrary loan (ILL), 42-43, 56, 66, 84, 96
interviews, 7, 89

John Cotton Dana Award, 93